National Hockey League

Official Rules

1999-2000

National Hockey League Official Rules 1999-2000

Printed in Canada.

Design, production by: Dan Diamond and Associates, Inc.
194 Dovercourt Road
Toronto, Ontario M6J 3C8
416/531-6535   Fax 416/531-3939

Distributed in Canada by: North 49 Books
35 Prince Andrew Drive
Toronto, Ontario M3C 2H2
416/449-4000   Fax 416/449-9924

Published in the United States of America by: Triumph Books
601 South LaSalle, Suite 500
Chicago, Illinois 60605
312/939-3330   Fax 312/663-3557

Cover photograph © courtesy of the Dallas Stars.

ISBN 1-57243-335-3

The National Hockey League
1251 Avenue of the Americas, New York, New York 10020-1198
1800 McGill College Avenue, Suite 2600, Montreal, Quebec H3A 3J6
50 Bay Street, 11th Floor, Toronto, Ontario M5J 2X8

NATIONAL HOCKEY LEAGUE
OFFICIAL RULES

TABLE OF CONTENTS

NOTE: "Commissioner" in these playing rules shall mean Commissioner of the National Hockey League or any League Officer designated by him to perform duties and exercise authority set out in these rules.

ALPHABETICAL INDEX

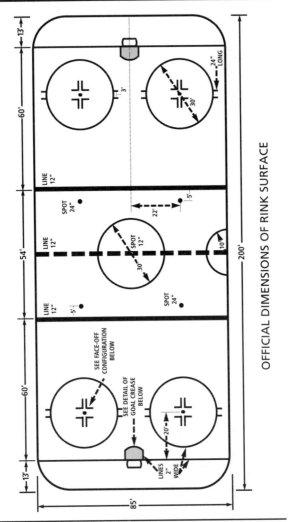

OFFICIAL DIMENSIONS OF RINK SURFACE

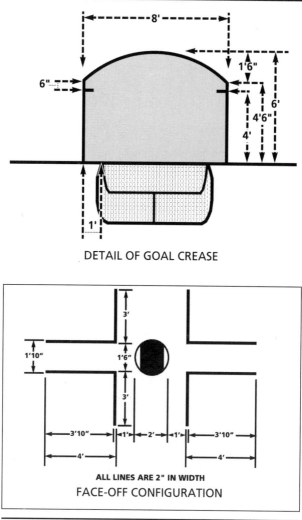

DETAIL OF GOAL CREASE

ALL LINES ARE 2" IN WIDTH

FACE-OFF CONFIGURATION

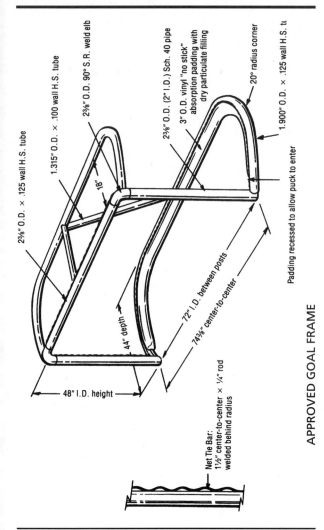

2⅜" O.D. × .125 wall H.S. tube

1.315" O.D. × .100 wall H.S. tube

2⅜" O.D. 90° S.R. weld elb

18"

2⅜" O.D. (2" I.D.) Sch. 40 pipe

3" O.D. vinyl "no stick" absorption padding with dry particulate filling

20° radius corner

1.900" O.D. × .125 wall H.S. tu

Padding recessed to allow puck to enter

44" depth

72" I.D. between posts

74⅜" center-to-center

48" I.D. height

APPROVED GOAL FRAME

Net Tie Bar: 1½" center-to-center × ¼" rod welded behind radius

RULES GOVERNING THE GAME OF ICE HOCKEY

SECTION ONE – THE RINK

Rule 1. Rink

The game of "Ice Hockey" shall be played on an ice surface known as the "RINK".

(NOTE) There shall be no markings on the ice except as provided under these rules without the express written permission of the League. On-ice logos must not interfere with any official game markings.

Rule 2. Dimensions of Rink

(a) The official size of the rink shall be two hundred feet (200') long and eighty-five feet (85') wide. The corners shall be rounded in the arc of a circle with a radius of twenty-eight feet (28').

The rink shall be surrounded by a wooden or fibreglass wall or fence known as the "boards" which shall extend not less than forty inches (40") and not more than forty-eight inches (48") above the level of the ice surface. The ideal height of the boards above the ice surface shall be forty-two inches (42"). Except for the official markings provided for in these rules, the entire playing surface and the boards shall be white in color except the kick plate at the bottom of the board which shall be light yellow in color.

Any variations from any of the foregoing dimensions shall require official authorization by the League.

(b) The boards shall be constructed in such a manner that the surface facing the ice shall be smooth and free of any obstruction or any object that could cause injury to players.

All doors giving access to the playing surface must swing away from the ice surface.

All glass or other types of protective screens and gear to hold them in position shall be properly padded or protected. Protective glass shall be required in front of the penalty benches to provide for the safety of the players on and off the ice. All equipment used to hold the glass or screens in position shall be mounted on the boards on the side away from the playing surface.

Rule 3. Goal Posts and Nets

(a) Thirteen feet (13') from each end of the rink and in the center of a red line two inches (2") wide drawn completely across the width of the ice and continued vertically up the side of the boards, regulation goal posts and nets shall be set in such a manner as to remain stationary during the progress of a game. The goal posts shall be kept in position by means of flexible pegs affixed in the ice or floor. The flexible pegs shall be eight inches (8") in length and yellow in color.

Where the length of the playing surface exceeds two hundred feet (200'), the goal line and goal posts may be placed not more than fifteen feet (15') from the end of the rink. The National Hockey League must grant prior approval.

(b) The goal posts shall be of approved design and material, extending vertically four feet (4') above the surface of the ice and set six feet (6') apart measured from the inside of the posts. A cross bar of the same material as the goal posts shall extend from the top of one post to the top of the other.

(c) There shall be attached to each goal frame a net of approved design made of white nylon cord which shall be draped in such a manner as to prevent the puck coming to rest on the outside of it, yet strung in a manner that will keep the puck in the net.

A skirt of heavy white nylon fabric or heavyweight white canvas shall be laced around the base plate of the goal frame in such a way as to protect the net from being cut or broken. This protective padding must be attached in a manner that will not restrict the puck from completely crossing the goal line. This skirt shall not project more than one inch (1") above the base plate.

(NOTE) The frame of the goal shall be draped with

*a nylon mesh net so as to completely enclose the
back of the frame. The net shall be made of three-
ply twisted twine (0.130 inch diameter) or
equivalent braided twine of multifilament white
nylon with an appropriate tensile strength of 700
pounds. The size of the mesh shall be two and one-
half inches (2½") (inside measurement) from
each knot to each diagonal knot when fully
stretched. Knotting shall be made as to ensure no
sliding of the twine. The net shall be laced to the
frame with medium white nylon cord no smaller in
size than No. 21.*

(d) The goal posts and cross bar shall be painted in
red and all other exterior surfaces shall be
painted in white.

(e) The red line, two inches (2") wide, between
the goal posts on the ice and extended
completely across the rink, shall be known as
the "GOAL LINE".

Rule 4. Goal Crease

(a) In front of each goal, a "GOAL CREASE" area
shall be marked by a red line two inches (2")
in width.

(b) The goal crease shall be laid out as follows:
One foot (1') outside of each goal post a two
inch (2") line shall be painted extending four
feet, six inches (4'6") in length. These lines
shall be at right angles to the goal line. A semi-
circle line six feet (6') in radius and two
inches (2") in width shall be drawn using the
center of the goal line as the center point and
connecting both ends of the side of the crease.

On the side of the crease lines, four feet (4')
from the goal line, extend a five-inch (5") line
into the crease. (see diagram on page 9)

(c) The goal crease area shall include all the space
outlined by the crease lines and extending
vertically four feet (4') to the level of the top
of the goal frame. The area outlined by the
crease line and the goal line shall be painted a
light blue color. (Paint code PMS 298.)

(d) The area inside the goal frame to the goal line
shall be painted a gloss white color.

Rule 5. Division of Ice Surface

(a) The ice area between the two goals shall be
divided into three parts by lines, twelve inches
(12") in width, and blue in color, drawn sixty
feet (60') out from the goal lines, and extended completely across the rink, parallel with
the goal lines, and continued vertically up the
side of the boards.

(b) That portion of the ice surface in which the
goal is situated shall be called the
"DEFENDING ZONE" of the Team defending
that goal; the central portion shall be known as
the "NEUTRAL ZONE", and the portion farthest
from the defended goal as the "ATTACKING
ZONE".

(c) There shall also be a line, twelve inches (12")
in width and red in color, drawn completely
across the rink in center ice, parallel with the
goal lines and continued vertically up the side

of the boards, known as the "CENTER LINE". This line shall contain regular interval markings of a uniform distinctive design, which will readily distinguish it from the two blue lines... the outer edges of which must be continuous.

Rule 6. Center Ice Spot and Circle

A circular blue spot, twelve inches (12") in diameter, shall be marked exactly in the center of the rink; and with this spot as a center, a circle of fifteen feet (15') radius shall be marked with a blue line two inches (2") in width.

Rule 7. Face-off Spots in Neutral Zone

Two red spots two feet (2') in diameter shall be marked on the ice in the neutral zone five feet (5') from each blue line. The spots shall be forty-four feet (44') apart and each shall be a uniform distance from the adjacent boards.

Rule 8. End Zone Face-off Spots and Circles

(a) In both end zones and on both sides of each goal, red face-off spots and circles shall be marked on the ice. The face-off spots shall be two feet (2') in diameter. Within the face-off spot, draw two parallel lines three inches (3") from the top and bottom of the spot. The area within the two lines shall be painted red, the remainder shall be painted white.

The circles shall be two inches (2") wide with a radius of fifteen feet (15') from the center of the face-off spots. At the outer edge of both sides of each face-off circle and parallel to the goal line shall be marked two red lines, two inches (2'') wide and two feet (2') in length and three feet (3') apart.

One foot away from the outer edge of the face-off spot, two lines shall be drawn parallel with the sideboards that shall be four feet (4')in length and eighteen inches (18") apart. Parallel to the end boards, commencing at the end of the line nearest to the face-off spot, a line shall extend two feet ten inches (2'10") in length. All lines shall be two inches (2") in width. (See diagram on page 9.)

(b) The location of the face-off spots shall be fixed in the following manner:

Along a line twenty feet (20') from each goal line and parallel to it, mark two points twenty-two feet (22') on both sides of the straight line joining the center of the two goals. Each such point shall be the center of a face-off spot and circle. (See diagram on page 8.)

Rule 9. Players' Benches

(a) Each rink shall be provided with seats or benches for the use of players of both Teams. The accommodations provided, including benches and doors, MUST be uniform for both Teams. Such seats or benches shall have accommodation for at least fourteen (14) persons of each Team. The benches shall be placed immediately alongside the ice as near to the center of the rink as possible. Two doors for each bench must be uniform in location and size and as convenient to the dressing rooms as possible.

Each players' bench should be twenty-four feet (24') in length and when situated in the spectator area, they shall be separated from the spectators by a protective glass of sufficient height so as to afford the necessary protection for the players. The players' benches shall be on the same side of the playing surface opposite the penalty bench and should be separated by a substantial distance, if possible.

> *(NOTE) Each players' bench shall have two doors which must be uniform in location and size. ("Mirrored image benches") All doors opening to the playing surface shall be constructed so that they swing inward.*

(b) No one but players in uniform, the Manager, Coach and Trainer shall be permitted to occupy the benches so provided.

> *(NOTE) One non-uniformed player shall be permitted on the players' bench in a coaching capacity. He must be indicated on the Roster Sheet submitted by the Coach to the Referee or Official Scorer prior to the start of the game in accordance with Rule 15 – Players in Uniform.*

Rule 10. Penalty Bench

(a) Each rink must be provided with benches or seats to be known as the "PENALTY BENCH". These benches or seats must be capable of accommodating a total of ten persons including the Penalty Timekeepers. Separate penalty benches shall be provided for each Team and they shall be situated on opposite sides of the Timekeeper's area, directly across the ice from the players' benches. The penalty bench(es) must be situated in the neutral zone.

(b) On the ice immediately in front of the Penalty Timekeeper's seat there shall be marked in red on the ice a semi-circle of ten foot (10') radius and two inches (2") in width which shall be known as the "REFEREE'S CREASE".

(c) Each Penalty Bench shall be protected from the spectator area by means of a glass partition which shall not be less than five feet (5') above the height of the boards.

Rule 11. Signal and Timing Devices

(a) Each rink must be provided with a siren, or other suitable sound device, for the use of Timekeepers.

(b) Each rink shall be provided with some form of electrical clock for the purpose of keeping the spectators, players and game officials accurately informed as to all time elements at all stages of the game including the time remaining to be played in any period and the time remaining to be served by at least five penalized players on each Team.

Time recording for both game time and

---

penalty time shall show time remaining to be played or served.

The game time clock shall measure the time remaining in tenths of a second during the last minutes of each period.

(c) Behind each goal, electrical lights shall be set up for the use of the Goal Judges. A red light will signify the scoring of a goal and a green light will signify the end of a period or a game.

> *(NOTE) A goal cannot be scored when a green light is showing.*

Rule 12. Police Protection

All clubs shall provide adequate police or other protection for all players and Officials at all times.

The Referee shall report to the Commissioner any failure of this protection observed by him or reported to him with particulars of such failure.

SECTION TWO – TEAMS

Rule 13. Composition of Team

(a) A Team shall be composed of six (6) players on the ice who shall be under contract to the Club they represent.

(b) Each player and each goalkeeper listed in the line-up of each Team shall wear an individual identifying number at least ten inches (10") high on the back of his sweater. Sweater numbers such as 00, ½ (fractions), .05 (decimals), 101 (three digit) are not permitted. In addition, each player and goalkeeper shall wear his surname in full, in block letters three inches (3") high, across the back of his sweater at shoulder height.

All players of each Team shall be dressed uniformly with approved design and color of their helmets, sweaters, short pants, stockings and skates.

Altered uniforms of any kind, i.e. velcro inserts, over-sized jerseys, etc. will not be permitted. Any player or goalkeeper not complying with this Rule shall not be permitted to participate in the game.

Each Member Club shall design and wear distinctive and contrasting uniforms for their home and road games, no parts of which shall be interchangeable except the pants.

Rule 14. Captain of Team

(a) One Captain shall be appointed by each Team,

and he alone shall have the privilege of discussing with the Referee any questions relating to interpretation of rules which may arise during the progress of a game. He shall wear the letter "C", approximately three inches (3") in height and in contrasting color, in a conspicuous position on the front of his sweater.

In addition, if the permanent Captain is not on the ice, Alternate Captains (not more than two) shall be accorded the privileges of the Captain. Alternate Captains shall wear the letter "A" approximately three inches (3") in height and in contrasting color, in a conspicuous position on the front of their sweaters.

(NOTE) Only when the captain is not in uniform, the Coach shall have the right to designate three Alternate Captains. This must be done prior to the start of the game.

(b) The Referee and Official Scorer shall be advised prior to the start of each game, the name of the Captain and the Alternate Captains of both Teams.

(c) Only the Captain, when invited to do so by the Referee, shall have the privilege of discussing any point relating to the interpretation of rules. Any Captain or player who comes off the bench and makes any protest or intervention with the Officials for any purpose may be assessed a misconduct penalty in addition to a minor penalty under Rule 41(b) – Abuse of Officials.

A complaint about a penalty is NOT a matter "relating to the interpretation of the rules" and a minor penalty shall be imposed against any Captain or other player making such a complaint.

(d) No playing Coach or playing Manager or goalkeeper shall be permitted to act as Captain or Alternate Captain.

Rule 15. Players in Uniform

(a) At the beginning of each game, the Manager or Coach of each Team shall list the players and goalkeepers who shall be eligible to play in the game. Not more than eighteen players, exclusive of goalkeepers, shall be permitted.

(b) A list of names and numbers of all eligible players and goalkeepers must be handed to the Referee or Official Scorer before the game, and no change shall be permitted in the list or addition thereto shall be permitted after the commencement of the game.

   i) If a goal is scored when an ineligible player is on the ice, the goal will be disallowed.

   ii) The ineligible player will be removed from the game and the club shall not be able to substitute another player on its roster.

(c) Each Team shall be allowed one goalkeeper on the ice at one time. The goalkeeper may be removed and another player substituted. Such substitute shall not be permitted the privileges of the goalkeeper.

(d) Each Team shall have on its bench, or on a chair immediately beside the bench, a substitute goalkeeper who shall, at all times, be fully dressed and equipped ready to play.

   The substitute goalkeeper may enter the game at any time following a stoppage of play, but no warm-up shall be permitted.

(e) Except when both goalkeepers are incapacitated, no player in the playing roster in that game shall be permitted to wear the equipment of the goalkeeper.

(f) In regular League and Playoff games, if both listed goalkeepers are incapacitated, that Team shall be entitled to dress and play any available goalkeeper who is eligible. This goalkeeper is eligible to sit on the player's bench, in uniform. No delay shall be permitted in taking his position in the goal, and he shall be permitted a two-minute warm-up. However, the warm-up is not permitted in the event a goalkeeper is substituted for a penalty shot.

(g) The Referee shall report to the Commissioner for disciplinary action any delay in making a substitution of goalkeepers.

Rule 16. Starting Line-Up

(a) Prior to the start of the game, at the request of the Referee, the Manager or Coach of the visiting Team is required to name the starting line-up to the Referee or Official Scorer. At any time in the game, at the request of the Referee made to the Captain, the visiting Team must place a playing line-up on the ice and promptly commence play.

(b) Prior to the start of the game, the Manager or Coach of the home Team, having been advised by the Official Scorer or the Referee the names of the starting line-up of the visiting Team, shall name the starting line-up of the home Team. This information shall be conveyed by the Official Scorer or the Referee to the Coach of the visiting Team.

(c) No change in the starting line-up of either Team as given to the Referee or Official Scorer, or in the playing line-up on the ice, shall be made until the game is actually in progress. For an infraction of this Rule, a bench minor penalty shall be imposed upon the offending Team, provided such infraction is called to the attention of the Referee before the second face-off in the first period takes place.

Rule 17. Change of Players

(a) Players may be changed at any time from the players' bench provided that the player or players leaving the ice shall be within five feet (5') of his players' bench and out of the play before the change is made.

A goalkeeper may be changed for another player at any time under conditions set out in this section.

(NOTE 1) When a goalkeeper or player of the Team in possession of the puck is substituted for prematurely, play shall be stopped immediately.

> *There shall be no time penalty to the Team making the premature substitution, but the resulting face-off will take place at the center ice face-off spot.*
>
> *In all other situations not covered in the above, a minor penalty may result for "too many men on the ice."*
>
> *(NOTE 2) The Referee shall request that the public address announcer make the following announcement: "Play has been stopped due to premature entry of a player from the players' bench." If in the course of making a substitution, the player entering the game plays the puck with his stick, skates or hands or who checks or makes any physical contact with an opposing player while the retiring player is actually on the ice, then the infraction of "too many men on the ice" will be called.*
>
> *If in the course of a substitution either the player entering the play or the player retiring is struck by the puck accidentally, the play will not be stopped and no penalty will be called.*

(b) If by reason of insufficient playing time remaining, or by reason of penalties already imposed, a bench minor penalty is imposed for deliberate illegal substitution (too many men on the ice) which cannot be served in its entirety within the legal playing time, or at any time in overtime, a penalty shot shall be awarded against the offending Team.

(c) A player serving a penalty on the penalty bench, who is to be changed after the penalty has been served, must proceed at once by way of the ice and be at his own players' bench before any change can be made.

For any violation of this Rule, a bench minor penalty shall be imposed.

(d) Following the stoppage of play, the visiting Team shall promptly place a line-up on the ice ready for play and no substitution shall be made from that time until play has been resumed. The home Team may then make any desired substitution which does not result in the delay of the game.

If there is any undue delay by either Team in changing lines, the Referee shall order the offending Team or Teams to take their positions immediately and not permit a line change.

(NOTE) When a substitution has been made under the above Rule, no additional substitution may be made until play commences.

(e) The Referee shall give the visiting Team a reasonable amount of time to make their change after which he shall put up his hand to indicate that no further change shall be made by the visiting club. At this point, the home Team may change immediately. Any attempt by the visiting Team to make a change after the Referee's signal shall result in the assessment of a bench minor penalty for delay of game.

Rule 18. Injured Players

(a) When a player other than a goalkeeper is injured or compelled to leave the ice during a game, he may retire from the game and be replaced by a substitute, but play must continue without the Teams leaving the ice.

(b) If a goalkeeper sustains an injury or becomes ill, he must be ready to resume play immediately or be replaced by a substitute goalkeeper and NO additional time shall be allowed by the Referee for the purpose of enabling the injured or ill goalkeeper to resume his position. The substitute goalkeeper shall be allowed a two (2) minute warm-up during all pre-season games. No warm-up shall be permitted for a substitute goalkeeper in all regular League or playoff games. (See also Section (d).)

(c) The Referee shall report to the Commissioner for disciplinary action any delay in making a goalkeeper substitution.

The substitute goalkeeper shall be subject to the regular rules governing goalkeepers and shall be entitled to the same privileges.

(d) When a substitution for the regular goalkeeper has been made, such regular goalkeeper shall not resume his position until the first stoppage of play thereafter.

(e) If a penalized player has been injured, he may proceed to the dressing room without the necessity of taking a seat on the penalty bench. If the injured player receives a minor penalty, the penalized Team shall immediately put a substitute player on the penalty bench, who shall serve the penalty without change. If the injured player receives a major penalty, the penalized Team shall place a substitute player on the penalty bench before the penalty expires and no other replacement for the penalized player shall be permitted to enter the game except from the penalty bench. For violation of this Rule, a bench minor penalty shall be imposed.

The injured penalized player who has been replaced on the penalty bench shall not be eligible to play until his penalty has expired.

(f) When a player is injured so that he cannot continue play or go to his bench, the play shall not be stopped until the injured player's Team has secured possession of the puck; if the player's Team is in possession of the puck at the time of injury, play shall be stopped immediately unless his Team is in a scoring position.

> *(NOTE) In the case where it is obvious that a player has sustained a serious injury, the Referee and/or Linesman may stop the play immediately.*

(g) When play has been stopped by the Referee or Linesman due to an injured player, such player must be substituted for immediately (except goalkeeper).

If when the attacking Team has control of the puck in its attacking zone, play is stopped by reason of any injury to a player of the defending Team, the face-off shall take place in the defending Team's end zone face-off spot.

SECTION THREE – EQUIPMENT

(NOTE 1) A request for a stick measurement shall be limited to one request per Team during the course of any stoppage in play.

(NOTE 2) Altered uniforms of any kind, e.g. Velcro inserts, over-sized jerseys, etc., will not be permitted. Any player or goalkeeper not complying with these Rules shall not be permitted to participate in the game.

NEW

(NOTE 3) These equipment regulations are written in the spirit of "fair play". If at any time the NHL feels that this spirit is being abused, the offending equipment will be deemed ineligible for play until a hearing has ruled on its eligibilty.

NEW

(NOTE 4) At random during the season, goalkeepers' and players' equipment shall be checked by League staff.

Rule 19. Sticks

(a) The sticks shall be made of wood or other material approved by the Rules Committee, and must not have any projections. Adhesive tape of any color may be wrapped around the stick at any place for the purpose of reinforcement or to improve control of the puck. In the case of a goalkeeper's stick, there shall be a knob of white tape or some other protective material approved by the League. This knob must not be less than one-half inch (½") thick at the top of the shaft.

Failure to comply with this provision of the Rule will result in the goalkeeper's stick being deemed unfit for play. The goalkeeper's stick must be changed without the application of a minor penalty.

(b) No stick shall exceed sixty-three inches (63")
in length from the heel to the end of the shaft
nor more than twelve and one-half inches
(12½") from the heel to the end of the blade.

The blade of the stick shall not be more
than three inches (3") in width at any point
nor less than two inches (2"). All edges of the
blade shall be beveled. The curvature of the
blade of the stick shall be restricted in such a
way that the distance of a perpendicular line
measured from a straight line drawn from any
point at the heel to the end of the blade to the
point of maximum curvature shall not exceed
one-half inch (½").

(c) The blade of the goalkeeper's stick shall not
exceed three and one-half inches (3½") in
width at any point except at the heel where it
must not exceed four and one-half inches
(4½") in width; nor shall the goalkeeper's
stick exceed fifteen and one-half inches
(15½") in length from the heel to the end of
the blade.

There is to be no measurement of the
curvature of the blade on the goalkeeper's
stick. All other elements of the stick are
subject to a measurement and the appropriate
applicable penalty.

The widened portion of the goalkeeper's
stick extending up the shaft from the blade
shall not extend more than twenty-six inches
(26") from the heel and shall not exceed three

and one-half inches (3½") in width.

(d) A minor penalty plus a fine of two hundred dollars ($200) shall be imposed on any player or goalkeeper who uses a stick not conforming to the provisions of this Rule.

> *(NOTE 1) When a formal complaint is made by the Captain or Alternate Captain of a Team, against the dimensions of any stick, the Referee shall take the stick to the Timekeeper's bench where the necessary measurement shall be made immediately. The result shall be reported to the Penalty Timekeeper who shall record it on the back of the penalty record.*
>
> *If the complaint is not sustained, a bench minor penalty shall be imposed against the complaining club in addition to a fine of one hundred dollars ($100).*
>
> *(NOTE 2) A player who participates in the play while taking a replacement stick to his goalkeeper shall incur a minor penalty under this Rule but the automatic fine of two hundred dollars ($200) shall not be imposed. If his participation causes a foul resulting in a penalty, the Referee shall report the incident to the Commissioner for disciplinary action.*
>
> *(NOTE 3) A request for a stick measurement in regular playing time or overtime is permitted. A request for a stick measurement following a goal in overtime is not permitted.*

(e) A minor penalty plus a ten (10) minute misconduct penalty shall be imposed on any player who refuses to surrender his stick for measurement when requested to do so by the Referee. In addition, this player shall be subject to a two hundred dollar ($200) fine.

Rule 20. Skates

(a) All hockey skates shall be of a design approved by the Rules Committee. All skates worn by players (but not goalkeepers) and by the Referee and Linesmen shall be equipped with an approved safety blade.

    When the Referee becomes aware that any person is wearing a skate that does not have the approved safety blade, he shall direct that it be replaced immediately. If such replacement is not carried out, the Referee shall report the incident to the Commissioner for disciplinary action.

(b) The use of speed skates or any skate so designed that it may cause injury is prohibited.

Rule 21. Goalkeeper's Equipment

(a) With the exception of skates and stick, all the equipment worn by the goalkeeper must be constructed solely for the purpose of protecting the head or body, and he must not wear any garment or use any contrivance which would give him undue assistance in keeping goal.

NEW

(b) The leg guards worn by goalkeepers shall not exceed twelve inches (12") in extreme width when on the leg of the player. No attachments such as plastic puck foils are permitted. Calf protectors must follow the contour of the calf and ankle and can have a thickness of no greater than one-and-one-half inches (1 ½").

NEW

(NOTE) These inspections can take place anytime, before, during, or after a game. A member of the League Staff (Hockey Operations and/or Security Departments) may obtain the equipment from any or all four participating goalkeepers. This equipment may be removed to a secure location for measuring.

Any violation of this Rule will result in an automatic one (1) game suspension for the next League game to the offending goalkeeper. Should both goalkeepers on a Club have illegal equipment, both will be suspended in sequence. The goalkeeper who played the day/night of the measurement will be suspended for the next game, and the back-up goalkeeper will be suspended for the following game.

NEW

The recalling of minor league goalkeepers to ensure a complete lineup for subsequent games, shall be deemed to be an Emergency Recall, and subject to the twenty-three (23) man roster limitations.

Refusal to submit the equipment for League measurement will result in the same sanctions as that of a goalkeeper with illegal equipment.

Any violation of this Rule shall be reported to the Club involved and to the Commissioner of the League.

(c) Chest and Arm Pads:

   (i) No raised ridges are allowed on the front edges or sides of the chest pad, the inside or outside of the arms, or across the shoulders.

NEW

   (ii) Layering at the elbow is permitted to add protection but not to add stopping area. This layering, both across the front and down the sides, to protect the point of the elbow shall not exceed seven-and-one-half inches (7 ½").

(iii) Shoulder Cap Protectors must follow the contour of the shoulder cap without becoming a projection/extension beyond or above the shoulder or shoulder cap. This contoured padding must not be more than one inch (1") in thickness beyond the top ridge of the shoulder and shoulder cap.

NEW

(iv) On each side the Shoulder Clavicle Protectors are not to exceed seven inches (7") in width. Their maximum thickness is to be one inch (1"). This protection is not to extend or project above or beyond the shoulder or shoulder cap nor extend beyond the armpit. No insert is allowed between the Shoulder Clavicle Protector and the chest pad that would elevate the Shoulder Clavicle Protector.

(v) If, when the goalie assumes his normal crouch position, the shoulder and/or shoulder cap protection is pushed above the contour of the shoulder, the chest pad will be considered illegal. (See Rule 23 (a) - Dangerous Equipment)

(d) Pants:

(i) No internal or external padding is permitted on the pant leg or waist other than to provide protection.

(ii) The maximum width (straight line) of the thigh pad across the front of the leg is eleven inches (11"). If the groin and/or hip

---

pads extend beyond the edge of the front thigh pad they are to be included in this eleven-inch measurement. This measurement is to be taken while the goalie is in an upright standing position. This measurement is to be made five inches (5") up from the bottom of the pant.

(e) Goalkeepers' Jerseys:

    (i)   The maximum jersey size is (see below).

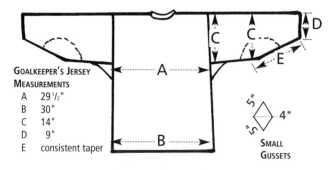

GOALKEEPER'S JERSEY MEASUREMENTS

A	29 1/2"
B	30"
C	14"
D	9"
E	consistent taper

SMALL GUSSETS

NEW

    (ii) No inserts or additions are to be added to the standard goalie cut jersey as produced by the manufacturer. (Modifications at the manufacturer are not allowed unless approved in advance by the League.) *(see Rule 13(b) – Composition of Team)*

    (iii) No "tying down" of the sweater is allowed at the wrists if it creates a tension across the jersey such that a "webbing effect" is created in the armpit area.

(iv) No other tie downs are allowed that created a "webbing effect."

(v) The length of a jersey is illegal if it covers any area between the goalies' legs.

(f) Catching glove

 (i) A maximum perimeter of forty-eight inches (48") is permitted. The perimeter of the glove is the distance around the glove. (See measurement procedures below)

(ii) The wrist cuff is to be a minimum of four-and-a-half inches (4 1/2") in height. The cuff of the glove is considered to be the portion of the glove protecting the wrist from the point where the thumb joint meets the wrist. Any protection joining/enhancing the cuff to the glove will be considered part of the glove rather than the cuff.

 (iii) The wrist cuff is to be a maximum of eight-and-one-half inches (8 ½") in width (this includes the bindings). All measurements follow the contour of the cuff.

 (iv) The distance from the heel of the glove along the pocket and following the contour of the inside of the trap of the glove to the top of the "T" trap must not exceed nineteen inches (19"). The heel is considered to be the point at which the straight vertical line from the cuff meets the glove (see diagram below).

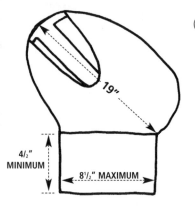

(v) Measuring Procedures for Goalkeepers' Catching Glove

(a) Suggested Equipment - binder clip, pins and a $5/8$" fiberglass cloth measuring tape that measures $1/8$ths of an inch.

(b) Procedure -

(1) The tape is to be placed on the outside edge of the glove with the midway line of the tape following the top ridge of the edge/binding.

(2) At the "starting point" of the measurement, anchor the tape with a pin or binder clip.

(3) Ensure that the midpoint line of the measuring tape follows the outside top ridge of the edge/binding.

(4) If at the junction of the cuff and catch portions of the glove there is a

"jagged point"; the measurement tape will follow the imaginary perpendicular line to the glove ridge above. (A "jagged joint" anywhere else on the glove will not be allowed this "straight line" privilege, i.e. where the trap joins the main glove).

(g) Blocking Glove

NEW

(i) Protective padding attached to the back or forming part of the goalkeeper's blocking glove shall not exceed eight inches (8") in width nor more than sixteen inches (16") in length at any point (this includes the bindings). All measurements follow the contour of the back of the glove.

NEW

(ii) The blocking glove must be rectangular in shape.

(h) Protective masks of a design approved by the Rules Committee may be worn by goalkeepers.

(NOTE) The Officiating Department is specifically authorized to make a check of each Teams' equipment to ensure the compliance with the Rule. It shall report its findings to the Commissioner for his disciplinary action.

Rule 22. Protective Equipment

(a) All protective equipment, except gloves, headgear and goalkeepers' leg guards must be worn under the uniform. For violation of this

Rule, after warning by the Referee, a minor
penalty shall be imposed.

> *(NOTE) Players including the goalkeeper violating
> this Rule shall not be permitted to participate in the
> game until such equipment has been corrected or
> removed.*

(b) All players of both Teams shall wear a helmet
of design, material and construction approved
by the Rules Committee at all times while
participating in a game, either on the playing
surface or the players' or penalty benches.

(c) A glove from which all or part of the palm has
been removed or cut to permit the use of the
bare hand shall be considered illegal equipment
and if any player wears such a glove in play, a
minor penalty shall be imposed on him.

When a complaint is made under this Rule, and
such complaint is not sustained, a bench minor
penalty shall be imposed against the complaining
club under Rule 51 – Delaying the Game.

Rule 23. Dangerous Equipment

(a) The use of pads or protectors made of metal, or
of any other material likely to cause injury to a
player, is prohibited.

> *(NOTE) All elbow pads which do not have a soft
> protective outer covering of sponge rubber or
> similar material at least one-half inch (1/2") thick
> shall be considered dangerous equipment.*

(b) A mask or protector of a design approved by
the Rules Committee may be worn by a player
who has sustained a facial injury.

In the first instance, the injured player shall be entitled to wear any protective device prescribed by the club doctor. If any opposing club objects to the device, it may record its objection with the Commissioner.

(NOTE) The Officiating Department is specifically authorized to make a check of each Team's equipment to ensure the compliance with this Rule. It shall report its findings to the Commissioner for his disciplinary action.

Rule 24. Puck

(a) The puck shall be made of vulcanized rubber, or other approved material, one inch (1") thick and three inches (3") in diameter and shall weigh between five and one-half ounces (5½ oz.) and six ounces (6 oz.). All pucks used in competition must be approved by the Rules Committee.

(b) The home Team shall be responsible for providing an adequate supply of official pucks which shall be kept in a frozen condition. This supply of pucks shall be kept at the penalty bench under the control of one of the regular Off-Ice Officials or a special attendant.

Rule 24A. Players' Jerseys

NEW

(a) The maximum jersey size is (see below).

(b) No inserts or additions are to be added to the standard players' jersey as produced by the manufacturer. (Modifications at the manufacturer are not allowed unless approved in advance by the League) (see

Rule 13(b) – Composition of Team).

(c) No alteration of the neck opening is permitted.

(d) Sleeves must extend into the cuff of the glove.

(e) Jerseys must be "tied down" properly at all times.

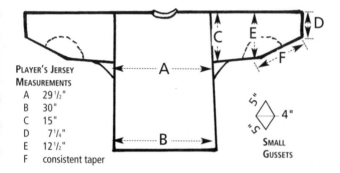

PLAYER'S JERSEY
MEASUREMENTS

A   29 1/2"
B   30"
C   15"
D   7 1/4"
E   12 1/2"
F   consistent taper

SMALL
GUSSETS

SECTION FOUR – PENALTIES

Rule 25. Penalties

Penalties shall be actual playing time and shall be divided in the following classes:

(1) Minor penalties

(2) Bench minor penalties

(3) Major penalties

(4) Misconduct penalties

(5) Match penalties

(6) Penalty shot

When coincident penalties are imposed on players of both Teams, the penalized players of the visiting Team shall take their positions on the penalty bench first in the place designated for visiting players.

(NOTE) When play is not actually in progress and an offense is committed by any player, the same penalty shall apply as though play was actually in progress.

Rule 26. Minor Penalties

(a) For a "MINOR PENALTY", any player, other than a goalkeeper, shall be ruled off the ice for two (2) minutes during which time no substitute shall be permitted.

(b) A "BENCH MINOR" penalty involves the removal from the ice of one player of the Team against which the penalty is assessed for a period of two (2) minutes. Any player except a goalkeeper of the Team may be designated to serve the penalty by the Manager or Coach through the playing Captain and such player shall take his place on the penalty bench promptly and serve the penalty as if it was a minor penalty imposed upon him.

(c) If while a Team is "short-handed" by one or more minor or bench minor penalties, the opposing Team scores a goal, the first of such penalties shall automatically terminate.

> *(NOTE) "Short-handed" means that the Team must be below the numerical strength of its opponents on the ice at the time the goal is scored. The minor or bench minor penalty which terminates automatically is the one with the least amount of time on the clock. Thus coincident minor penalties to both Teams do NOT cause either side to be "short-handed".*
>
> *This Rule shall also apply when a goal is scored on a penalty shot, or when an awarded goal is given.*
>
> **Minor penalty expiration criteria:**
> > *i) Is the Team scored against short handed?*
> > *ii) Is the Team scored against serving a Minor Penalty on the clock?*
>
> *If both criteria are satisfied, the minor penalty with the least amount of time on the clock shall terminate except when coincidental penalties are being served.*

When the minor penalties of two players of the same Team terminate at the same time, the Captain of that Team shall designate to the Referee which of such players will return to the ice first and the Referee will instruct the Penalty Timekeeper accordingly.

When a player receives a major penalty and a minor penalty at the same time, the major penalty shall be served first by the penalized player, except under Rule 27(c) in which case the minor penalty will be recorded and served first.

> *(NOTE) This applies to the case where BOTH penalties are imposed on the SAME player. See also Note to Rule 32.*

(d) When ONE minor penalty is assessed to ONE player of EACH Team at the same stoppage in play, these penalties will be served without substitution provided there are no other penalties in effect and visible on the penalty clocks.

Unless paragraph one of this Rule is applicable, when coincident minor penalties or coincident minor penalties of equal duration are imposed against players of both Teams, the penalized players shall all take their places on the penalty benches and such penalized players shall not leave the penalty bench until the first stoppage of play following the expiry of their respective penalties. Immediate substitution shall be made for an equal number of minor penalties OR coincident minor penalties of equal duration to each Team so penalized and the penalties of the players for which substitutions have been made shall not be taken into account for the purpose of the Delayed Penalty Rule (Rule 32).

Rule 27. Major Penalties

(a) For the first "MAJOR PENALTY" in any one game, the offender, except the goalkeeper, shall be ruled off the ice for five (5) minutes during which time no substitute shall be permitted.

An automatic fine of one hundred dollars ($100) shall also be added when a major penalty is imposed for any foul causing injury to the face or head of an opponent by means of a stick.

(b) For the third major penalty in the same game to the same player, or for a major for butt-ending, checking from behind, clipping, cross-checking, hooking, slashing or spearing, he shall be ruled off the ice for the balance of the game, but a substitute shall be permitted to replace the player so suspended after five (5) minutes have elapsed. (Major penalty plus game misconduct with automatic fine of two hundred dollars ($200).)

(c) When coincident major penalties or coincident penalties of equal duration, including a major penalty, are imposed against players of both Teams, the penalized players shall all take their places on the penalty benches and such penalized players shall not leave the penalty benches until the first stoppage of play following the expiry of their respective penalties. Immediate substitutions shall be made for an equal number of major penalties, or coincident penalties of equal duration including a major penalty to each Team so penalized, and the penalties of the players for which substitutions have been made shall not be taken into account for the purpose of the Delayed Penalty Rule, (Rule 32).

Where it is required to determine which of the penalized players shall be designated to serve the delayed penalty under Rule 32 – Delayed Penalties, the penalized Team shall have the right to make such designation not in conflict with Rule 26 – Minor Penalties.

(d) During the last five (5) minutes of regulation time, or at any time in overtime, when a minor penalty and a major penalty are assessed to two opposing players on the same stoppage of play, the three-minute differential shall be served immediately as a major penalty. This is also applicable when coincidental penalties are negated, leaving the aforementioned example. In such instances, the Team of the player receiving the major penalty must place the replacement player in the penalty bench prior to expiration of the penalty. The differential will be recorded on the penalty clock as a three (3) minute penalty, and served in the same manner as a major penalty.

Rule 28. Misconduct Penalties

(a) In the event of
"MISCONDUCT"
penalties to any
players except the
goalkeeper, the
players shall be
ruled off the ice for
a period of ten (10)
minutes each. A
substitute player is
permitted to
immediately replace
a player serving a

MISCONDUCT
Place both hands on hips

misconduct penalty. A player whose
misconduct penalty has expired shall remain
in the penalty box until the next stoppage of
play.

When a player receives a minor penalty and
a misconduct penalty at the same time, the
penalized Team shall immediately put a
substitute player on the penalty bench and he
shall serve the minor penalty without change.

When a player receives a major penalty and
a misconduct penalty at the same time, the
penalized Team shall place a substitute player
on the penalty bench before the major penalty
expires and no replacement for the penalized
player shall be permitted to enter the game
except from the penalty bench. Any violation of
this provision shall be treated as an illegal

substitution under Rule 17 calling for a bench minor penalty.

(b) A misconduct penalty imposed on any player at any time shall be accompanied with an automatic fine of one hundred dollars ($100).

(c) A "GAME MISCONDUCT" penalty involves the suspension of a player for the balance of the game but a substitute is permitted to replace immediately the player so removed. A player incurring a game misconduct penalty shall incur an automatic fine of two hundred dollars ($200) and the case shall be reported to the Commissioner who shall have full power to impose such further penalties by way of suspension or fine on the penalized player or any other player involved in the altercation.

(d) The Referee may impose a "GROSS MISCONDUCT" penalty on any player, Manager, Coach or Trainer who is guilty of gross misconduct of any kind. Any person incurring a "gross misconduct" penalty shall be suspended for the balance of the game and shall incur an automatic fine of two hundred dollars ($200) and the case shall be referred to the Commissioner of the League for further disciplinary action.

> *(NOTE) For all game misconduct and gross misconduct penalties regardless of when imposed, a total of ten minutes shall be charged in the records against the offending player.*

(e) In regular League games, any player who incurs a total of three (3) game misconduct penalties in the "General Category" and exclusive of other designated categories, shall be suspended for the next League game of his Team. For each subsequent game misconduct penalty, the automatic suspension shall be increased by one game. For each suspension of a player, his Club shall be fined one thousand dollars ($1,000).

In Playoff games, any player who incurs a total of two game misconduct penalties shall be suspended automatically for the next Playoff game of his Team. For each subsequent game misconduct penalty during the Playoffs, the automatic suspension shall be increased by one game. For each suspension of a player during Playoffs, his club shall be fined one thousand dollars ($1,000).

(f) In regular League or Playoff games, any player who incurs a total of two (2) game misconduct penalties for Abuse of Officials related infractions penalized under Rule 41(b) Abuse of Officials and other Misconduct, shall be suspended automatically for the next League or Playoff game of his Team. For each subsequent game misconduct penalty, the automatic suspension shall be increased by one game.

(g) In regular League games, any player who incurs a total of two (2) game misconduct penalties for stick related infractions penalized under Rule 27(b) shall be suspended automatically for the next League game of his Team. For each subsequent game misconduct penalty, the automatic suspension shall be increased by one game.

In playoff games any player who incurs a total of two (2) game misconduct penalties for stick related infractions penalized under Rule 27(b) shall be suspended automatically for the next Playoff game of his Team. For each subsequent game misconduct penalty during the Playoffs the automatic suspension shall be increased by one game.

Prior to the commencement of each Stanley Cup Finals, a player will have his current stick-related, boarding and checking from behind game misconducts removed from his current playoff record. They will remain part of his historical record.

(NOTE 1) Any game misconduct penalty for which a player has been assessed an automatic suspension or supplementary discipline in the form of game suspension(s) by the Commissioner shall NOT be taken into account when calculating the total number of offenses under this subsection.

(NOTE 2) When a player has played in 41 consecutive regular League games without being assessed a stick-related major and a game misconduct according to Rule 27(b) – Major Penalties or Rule 28 (f) – Misconduct Penalties, he will have the previous game misconduct penalties removed from his current record. They will remain part of his historical record.

(NOTE 3) When a player has played in 41

---

consecutive regular League games without being assessed a boarding and/or a checking from behind major and a game misconduct according to Rule 44 – Boarding and Rule 48 – Checking from Behind, he will have the previous game misconduct penalties removed from his current record. They will remain part of his historical record.

(NOTE 4) A player's total games played will cover a two year time period from the date of the first game misconduct penalty for each category of foul.

(NOTE 5) The automatic suspensions incurred under this subsection in respect to League games shall have no effect with respect to violations during playoff games.

Rule 29. Match Penalties

A "MATCH" penalty involves the suspension of a player for the balance of the game and the offender shall be ordered to the dressing room immediately. A substitute player is permitted to replace the penalized player after five (5) minutes playing time has elapsed when the penalty is imposed under Rule 43 – Attempt to Injure or Rule 52 – Deliberate Injury of Opponents.

(NOTE 1) Regulations regarding additional penalties and substitutes are specifically covered in individual Rules 43, 52 and 69. Any additional penalty shall be served by a player to be designated by the Manager or Coach of the offending Team through the playing Captain, such player to take his place in the penalty box immediately.

For all match penalties, regardless of when imposed, or prescribed additional penalties, a total of ten minutes shall be charged in the records against the offending player.

(NOTE 2) When coincident match penalties have been imposed under Rule 43, Rule 52 or Rule 69 to a player on both Teams, Rule 27(c) covering coincident major penalties will be applicable with respect to player substitution.

(NOTE 3) The Referee is required to report all match penalties and the surrounding circumstances to the Commissioner of the League immediately following the game in which they occur.

Rule 30. Penalty Shot

(a) Any infraction of the rules which calls for a "PENALTY SHOT" shall be taken as follows:

The Referee shall ask to have announced over the public address system the name of the player designated by him or selected by the Team entitled to take the shot (as appropriate). He shall then place the puck on the center face-off spot and the player taking the shot will, on the instruction of the Referee, play the puck from there and shall attempt to score on the goalkeeper. The player taking the shot may carry the puck in any part of the neutral zone or his own defending zone but once the puck has crossed the attacking blue line it must be kept in motion towards the opponent's goal line and once it is shot, the play shall be considered complete. No goal can be scored on a rebound of any kind (an exception being the puck off the goal post, then the goalkeeper and then directly into the goal), and any time the puck crosses the goal line, the shot shall be considered complete.

Only a player designated as a goalkeeper or alternate goalkeeper may defend against the penalty shot.

(b) The goalkeeper must remain in his crease until the player taking the penalty shot has touched the puck and in the event of violation of this Rule or any foul committed by a goalkeeper, the Referee shall allow the shot to be taken and if the shot fails, he shall permit the penalty shot to be taken over again.

The goalkeeper may attempt to stop the shot in any manner except by throwing his stick or any object, in which case a goal shall be awarded.

(NOTE) See Rule 88.

(c) In cases where a penalty shot has been awarded under Rule 51(c), deliberately displacing goal post during course of a breakaway; under Rule 67(i), Interference; under Rule 72(m), illegal entry into the game; under Rule 88(a) for throwing a stick; and under Rule 91(b), fouling from behind, the Referee shall designate the player who has been fouled as the player who shall take the penalty shot.

In cases where a penalty shot has been awarded under Rule 17(b), deliberate illegal substitution with insufficient playing time remaining; under Rule 51(d), deliberately displacing goal post; under Rule 55(c), falling on the puck in the crease; under Rule 59(d), picking up the puck from the crease area, the penalty shot shall be taken by a player selected by the Captain of the non-offending Team from the players on the ice at the time when the foul was committed. Such selection shall be reported to the Referee and cannot be changed.

If by reason of injury, the player designated by the Referee to take the penalty shot is unable to do so within a reasonable time, the shot may be taken by a player selected by the Captain of the non-offending Team from the players on the ice when the foul was committed. Such selection shall be reported to the Referee and cannot be changed.

(d) Should the player in respect to whom a penalty shot has been awarded himself commit a foul in connection with the same play or circumstances, either before or after the penalty shot has been awarded, be designated to take the shot, he shall first be permitted to do so before being sent to the penalty bench to serve the penalty except when such penalty is for a game misconduct, gross misconduct or match penalty in which case the penalty shot shall be taken by a player selected by the Captain of the non-offending Team from the players on the ice at the time when the foul was committed.

If at the time a penalty shot is awarded, the goalkeeper of the penalized Team has been removed from the ice to substitute another player, the goalkeeper shall be permitted to return to the ice before the penalty shot is taken.

(e) While the penalty shot is being taken, players of both sides shall withdraw to the sides of the rink and in front of their own player's bench.

(f) If, while the penalty shot is being taken, any player of the opposing Team shall have by some action interfered with or distracted the player taking the shot and, because of such action, the shot should have failed, a second attempt shall be permitted and the Referee shall impose a misconduct penalty on the player so interfering or distracting.

(g) If a goal is scored from a penalty shot, the puck shall be faced-off at center ice. If a goal is not scored, the puck shall be faced-off at either of the end face-off spots in the zone in which the penalty shot was tried.

(h) Should a goal be scored from a penalty shot, a further penalty to the offending player shall not be applied unless the offense for which the penalty shot was awarded was such as to incur a major, match or misconduct penalty, in which case the penalty prescribed for the particular offense shall be imposed.

If the offense for which the penalty shot was awarded was such as to normally incur a minor penalty, then regardless of whether the penalty shot results in a goal or not, no further minor penalty shall be served.

If the offense for which the penalty shot was awarded was such as to incur a double minor penalty, the scoring of a goal on a penalty shot shall negate one minor only of the double minor penalty to be joriginally assessed.

(i) If the foul upon which the penalty shot is based occurs during actual playing time, the penalty shot shall be awarded and taken immediately in the usual manner not-withstanding any delay occasioned by a slow whistle by the Referee to permit the play to be completed, which delay results in the expiry of the regular playing time in any period.

The time required for the taking of a penalty shot shall not be included in the regular playing time or overtime.

(j) If, after a player's stick has been ruled illegal, he attempts to take a penalty shot with a second stick that is also ruled illegal prior to taking the penalty shot, the opportunity to take the penalty shot shall be disallowed. The player shall be assessed one minor penalty for the first illegal stick.

Rule 31. Goalkeeper's Penalties

(a) A goalkeeper shall not be sent to the penalty bench for an offense which incurs a minor penalty, but instead, the minor penalty shall be served by another member of his Team who was on the ice when the offense was committed. This player is to be designated by the Manager or Coach of the offending Team through the playing Captain and such substitute shall not be changed.

> *(NOTE) A penalized player may not serve a goalkeeper's penalty.*

(b) A goalkeeper shall not be sent to the penalty bench for an offense which incurs a major penalty, but instead, the major penalty shall be served by another member of his Team who was on the ice when the offense was committed. This player is to be designated by the Manager or Coach of the offending Team through the playing Captain and such substitute shall not be changed.

(c) Should a goalkeeper incur three major penalties in one game, in accordance with Rule 27(b) – Major Penalties, he shall be ruled off the ice for the balance of the playing time and his place shall be taken by a member of his own club, or by a regular substitute goalkeeper who is available. Such player will be allowed the goalkeeper's equipment. (Major penalty plus game misconduct penalty and automatic fine of two hundred dollars ($200).)

(d) Should a goalkeeper on the ice incur a misconduct penalty, this penalty shall be served by another member of his Team who was on the ice when the offense was committed. This player is to be designated by the Manager or Coach of the offending Team through the Captain and, in addition, the goalkeeper shall be fined one hundred dollars ($100).

(e) Should a goalkeeper incur a game misconduct penalty, his place will then be taken by a member of his own club, or by a regular substitute goalkeeper who is available, and such player will be allowed the goalkeeper's full equipment. In addition, the goalkeeper shall be fined two hundred dollars ($200).

(f) Should a goalkeeper incur a match penalty, his place will then be taken by a member of his own club, or by a substitute goalkeeper who is available, and such player will be allowed the goalkeeper's full equipment. However, any additional penalties as specifically called for by the individual rules covering match penalties will apply, and the offending Team shall be penalized accordingly. Such additional penalties will be served by other members of the Team on the ice when the offenses were committed. These players are to be designated by the Manager or Coach of the offending Team through the Captain. (See Rules 43, 52 and 69.)

(g) Should a goalkeeper incur a match penalty, the case shall be investigated promptly by the Commissioner who shall have full power to fine or suspend the penalized goalkeeper or any other players in the altercation.

(h) A minor penalty shall be imposed on a goalkeeper who leaves the immediate vicinity of his crease during an altercation. In addition, he shall be subject to a fine of two hundred dollars ($200) and this incident shall be reported to the Commissioner for such further disciplinary action as may be required.

> *(NOTE) All penalties imposed on a goalkeeper, regardless of who serves the penalty or any substitution, shall be charged in the records against the goalkeeper.*

(i) If a goalkeeper participates in the play in any manner when he is beyond the center red line, a minor penalty shall be imposed upon him.

Rule 32. Delayed Penalties

(a) If a third player of any Team shall be penalized while two players of the same Team are serving penalties, the penalty time of the third player shall not commence until the penalty time of one of the two players already penalized has elapsed. Nevertheless, the third player penalized must at once proceed to the penalty bench but may be replaced by a substitute until such time as the penalty time of the penalized player shall commence.

(b) When any Team shall have three players serving penalties at the same time and because of the delayed penalty rule, a substitute for the third offender is on the ice, none of the three penalized players on the penalty bench may return to the ice until play has stopped. When play has been stopped, the player whose full penalty has expired may return to the play.

DELAYED CALLING OF PENALTY
Referee extends arm and points to penalized player.

Provided however that the Penalty Timekeeper shall permit the return to the ice in the order of expiry of their penalties, of a player or players when, by reason of the expiration of their penalties, the penalized Team is entitled to have more than four players on the ice.

(c) In the case of delayed penalties, the Referee shall instruct the Penalty Timekeeper that penalized players whose penalties have expired shall only be allowed to return to the ice when there is a stoppage of play.

When the penalties of two players of the same Team will expire at the same time, the Captain of that Team will designate to the Referee which of such players will return to the ice first and the Referee will instruct the Penalty Timekeeper accordingly.

When a major and a minor penalty are imposed at the same time on players of the same Team, the Penalty Timekeeper shall record the minor as being the first of such penalties.

(NOTE) This applies to the case where the two penalties are imposed on DIFFERENT players of the same Team. See also Note to Rule 26 – Minor Penalties.

Rule 33. Calling of Penalties

(a) Should an infraction of the rules which would call for a minor, major, misconduct, game misconduct or match penalty be committed by a player of the side in possession of the puck, the Referee shall immediately blow his whistle and penalize the offending player.

The resulting face-off shall be made at the place where the play was stopped unless the stoppage occurs in the attacking zone of the player penalized in which case the face-off shall be made at the nearest face-off spot in the neutral zone.

(b) Should an infraction of the rules which would call for a minor, major, misconduct, game misconduct or match penalty be committed by a player of the Team not in possession of the puck, the Referee will blow his whistle and impose the penalty on the offending player upon completion of the play by the Team in possession of the puck.

(NOTE) There shall be no signal given by the Referee for a misconduct or game misconduct penalty under this section.

The resulting face-off shall be made at the place where the play was stopped, unless during the period of a delayed whistle due to a foul by a player of the side NOT in possession, the side in possession ices the puck, shoots the puck so that it goes out of bounds or is unplayable, then the face-off following the stoppage shall take place in the neutral zone near the defending blue line of the Team shooting the puck.

If the penalty to be imposed is a minor penalty and a goal is scored on the play by the non-offending side, the minor penalty shall not be imposed but major and match penalties shall be imposed in the normal manner regardless of whether or not a goal is scored.

When the penalty to be imposed is applicable under Rule 46 (a) – Butt-Ending; Rule 60(a) – Head-Butting; Rule 61(c)(1) – High Sticks or Rule 86(a) – Spearing, and a goal is scored, two minutes of the appropriate penalty will be assessed to the offending player. (This will be announced as a double minor for the appropriate foul and the player will serve two (2) minutes only.)

If when a Team is "short-handed" by reason of one or more minor or bench minor penalties, the Referee signals a further minor penalty or penalties against the "short-handed" Team and a goal is scored by the non-offending side before the whistle is blown, then the goal shall be allowed. The penalty or penalties signalled

shall be assessed and the first of the minor
penalties already being served shall
automatically terminate under Rule 26(c) –
Minor Penalties. Major and match penalties
shall be imposed in the normal manner
regardless of whether or not a goal is scored.

*(NOTE 1) "Completion of the play by the Team in
possession" in this Rule means that the puck must
have come into the possession and control of an
opposing player or has been "frozen". This does not
mean a rebound off the goalkeeper, the goal or the
boards, or any accidental contact with the body or
equipment of an opposing player.*

*(NOTE 2) If after the Referee has signalled a
penalty but before the whistle has been blown, the
puck shall enter the goal of the non-offending Team
as the direct result of a player of that Team, the
goal shall be allowed and the penalty signalled
shall be imposed in the normal manner.*

(c) Should the same offending player commit
other fouls on the same play, either before or
after the Referee has blown his whistle, the
offending player shall serve such penalties
consecutively.

Rule 33A. Supplementary Discipline

In addition to the automatic fines and
suspensions imposed under these Rules, the
Commissioner may, at his discretion,
investigate any incident that occurs in
connection with any Pre-season, Exhibition,
League or Playoff game and may assess
additional fines and/or suspensions for any

offense committed during the course of a game or any aftermath thereof by a player, Trainer, Manager, Coach or club executive, whether or not such offense has been penalized by the Referee.

> *(NOTE) If an investigation is requested by a Club or by the League on its own initiative, it must be initiated within twenty-four (24) hours following the completion of the game in which the incident occurred.*

Rule 33B.   Suspensions Arising from Pre-season and Exhibition Games

Whenever suspensions are imposed as a result of infractions occurring during pre-season and exhibition games, the Commissioner shall exercise his discretion in scheduling the suspensions to ensure that no Team shall be short more players in any regular League game than it would have been had the infractions occurred in regular League games.

SECTION FIVE – OFFICIALS

Rule 34. Appointment of Officials

(a) The Commissioner shall appoint one or two Referees (as appropriate), two Linesmen, Game Timekeeper, Official Scorer, two Goal Judges and a Video Goal Judge for each game.

(b) The Commissioner shall forward to all clubs a list of Referees, Linesmen, and Off-Ice Officials, all of whom must be treated with proper respect at all times during the season by all players and officials of clubs.

Rule 35. Referee

(a) The Referee(s) shall have general supervision of the game and shall have full control of all game officials and players during the game, including stoppages; and in case of any dispute, his decision shall be final. The Referee shall remain on the ice at the conclusion of each period until all players have proceeded to their dressing rooms.

(b) All Referees and Linesmen shall be dressed in black trousers and official sweaters.

They shall be equipped with approved whistles, tape measure and an official stick measuring gauge.

(c) The Referee(s) shall order the Teams on the ice at the appointed time for the beginning of a game and at the commencement of each period. If for any reason, there is more than

---

fifteen (15) minutes' delay in the commencement of the game or any undue delay in
resuming play after the fifteen-minute
intervals between periods, the Referee shall
state in his report to the Commissioner the
cause of the delay and the club or clubs which
were at fault.

(d) It shall be his duty to see to it that all players
are properly dressed, and that the approved
regulation equipment (including the approved
on-ice branded exposure program) is in use at
all times during the game.

(e) The Referee(s) shall, before starting the game,
see that the appointed Game Timekeeper,
Penalty Timekeeper, Official Scorer and Goal
Judges are in their respective places and
ensure that the timing and signalling
equipment are in order.

(f) It shall be his duty to impose such penalties as
are prescribed by the rules for infractions
thereof and he shall give the final decision in
matters of disputed goals. The Referee may
consult with the Linesmen, Goal Judge or
Video Goal Judge before making his decision.

(g) The Referee shall announce to the Official
Scorer regarding the legality of an apparent
goal. The Official Scorer, with the assistance of
the Video Goal Judge, will confirm the goal
scorer and any players deserving of an assist.
See also Rule 57 (Note) – Goals and Assists.

The Referee shall have announced over the public address system the reason for not allowing a goal every time the goal signal light is turned on in the course of play. This shall be done at the first stoppage of play regardless of any standard signal given by the Referee when the goal signal light was put on in error.

The Referee shall report to the Official Scorer the name or number of the goal scorer but he shall not give any information or advice with respect to assist.

(NOTE) The name of the scorer and any player entitled to an assist will be announced on the public address system. In the event that the Referee disallows a goal for any violation of the rules, he shall report the reason for disallowance to the Official Scorer who shall announce the Referee's decision correctly over the public address system.

The infraction of the rules for which each penalty has been imposed will be announced correctly, as reported by the Referee, over the public address system. Where players of both Teams are penalized on the same play, the penalty to the visiting player will be announced first.

Where a penalty is imposed by the Referee which calls for a mandatory or automatic fine, only the time portion of the penalty will be reported by the Referee to the Official Scorer and announced on the public address system, and the fine will be collected through the League office.

(h) The Referee shall see to it that players of opposing Teams are separated on the penalty bench to prevent feuding.

(i) He shall not halt the game for any infractions of the rules concerning off-side play at the blue line or center line, or any violation of Rule 65, icing the puck. Determining infractions of these rules is the duty of the Linesmen unless, by virtue of some accident, the Linesman is prevented from doing so in which case the duties of the Linesman shall be assumed by the Referee until play is stopped.

(j) Should a Referee accidentally leave the ice or receive an injury which incapacitates him from discharging his duties while play is in progress, the game shall be automatically stopped.

(k) If, through misadventure or sickness, the Referee and Linesmen appointed are prevented from appearing, the Managers or Coaches of the two clubs shall agree on a Referee and Linesman. If they are unable to agree, they shall appoint a player from each side who shall act as Referee and Linesman; the player of the home club acting as Referee and the player of the visiting club as Linesman.

(l) If the regularly appointed Officials appear during the progress of the game, they shall at once replace the temporary Officials.

(m) Should a Linesman appointed be unable to act at the last minute or through sickness or accident be unable to finish the game, the Referee shall have the power to appoint another in his stead, if he deems it necessary, or if required to do so by the Manager or Coach of either of the competing Teams.

(n) If, owing to illness or accident, the Referee (or one Referee in a Two Referee game) is unable to continue to officiate, one of the Linesmen (or the remaining Referee in a Two Referee game) shall perform the duties of the ill or injured Referee during the balance of the game. If a Linesman is to be assigned the Referee or Officiating Supervisor will select him. In the event that an NHL Supervisor is in attendance at a game where a spare Official is present, he shall have the authority to substitute the injured Referee with the spare Official.

(o) The Referee shall check club rosters and all players in uniform before signing reports of the game.

(p) The Referee shall report to Commissioner promptly and in detail the circumstances of any of the following incidents:

   (i) When a stick or part thereof is thrown outside the playing area – Rule 88(c) – Throwing Stick;

   (ii) Every obscene gesture made by any person involved in the playing or conduct of the game whether as a participant or as an official of either Team or of the League, which gesture he has personally observed or which has been brought to his attention by any game official – Rule 73(a) – Obscene or Profane Language or Gestures;

(iii) When any player, Trainer, Coach or club executive becomes involved in an altercation with a spectator – Rule 68(b) – Interference by/with Spectators;

(iv) Every infraction under Rule 27(b) – Major Penalties, major and game misconducts.

(q) In the event of failure by a club to comply with a provision of the League constitution, by-laws, resolutions, rules or regulations affecting the playing of a game, the Referee shall, if so directed by the Commissioner or his designee, refuse to permit the game to proceed until the offending club comes into compliance with such provision.

Should the offending club persist in its refusal to come into compliance, the Referee shall, with the prior approval of the Commissioner or his designee, declare the game forfeited and the non-offending club the winner. Should the Referee declare the game forfeited because both clubs have refused to comply with such a provision, the visiting club shall be declared the winner.

If the game is declared forfeited prior to its having commenced, the score shall be recorded as 1-0 and no player shall be credited with any personal statistics.

If the game was in progress at the time it is declared forfeited, the score shall be recorded as zero for the loser and 1, or such greater number of goals that had been scored by it, for the winner; however, the players on both clubs shall be credited with all personal statistics earned up to the time the forfeit was declared.

(r) In the event of any dispute regarding time or the expiration of penalties, the matter shall be referred to the Referee for adjustment and his decision shall be final. He may use the Video Goal Judge to assist in rendering the final decision. (See Rule 93 (g) – Video Goal Judge.

Rule 36. Linesman

(a) The Linesman shall stop play:

1. When premature substitution of the goalkeeper or player has occurred: Rule 17(a) – Change of Players.

2. When he deems that a player has sustained a serious injury: Rule 18(f) – Injured Players.

3. When the goal post has been displaced from its normal position: Rule 51 – Delaying the Game.

4. For premature entry into the face-off area: Rule 54(a)(e) – Face-offs.

5. When the puck has been deliberately hand passed to a Teammate in any zone other than the defensive zone: Rule 59(e) – Handling the Puck with Hands.

6. When the puck is struck above the height of the shoulders: Rule 61(d) High Sticks.

7. For violation of icing the puck: Rule 65 – Icing

the Puck.

8. When there has been interference by/with spectators: Rule 68 – Interference by/with Spectators.

9. For any infraction of the rules concerning off-side play at the blue line: Rule 74 – Off-Sides.

10. For any infraction of the rules concerning off-side at the red line: Rule 75 – Passes or at the blue line: Rule 77 – Preceding Puck into the Attacking Zone.

11. When the puck is out of bounds or unplayable: Rule 80 – Puck Out of Bounds or Unplayable.

12. When a goal has been scored that has not been observed by the Referee.

13. When the puck is interfered with by an ineligible player/person.

14. The calling of a penalty shot under Rule 88(a) – Throwing Stick.

The Linesman may stop play and assess a minor penalty for:

1. Too many men on the ice: Rule 17 – Change of Players.

2. Articles thrown on the ice from the players' bench or penalty bench: Rule 41(k) – Abuse of Officials and Other Misconduct.

3. (Bench minor) when Team personnel interfere with a game official: Rule 41(l) – Abuse of Officials and Other Misconduct.

4. Receiving an illegal stick from players' bench or penalty bench: Rule 45(c) – Broken Stick.

5. Delay of game by deliberately displacing

goal post: Rule 51(c) – Delaying the Game.

6. The instigation of an incident by a player of the opposing Team for which a major/match penalty was assessed following the original incident. The Linesman will report this to the Referee.

The Linesman may stop play and assess a double minor for:

1. Butt-ending: Rule 46(a) – Butt-ending.
2. Head-butting: Rule 60(a) – Head-butting
3. High-sticking: Rule 61(b) – High Sticks
4. Spearing: Rule 86(a) – Spearing.

The Linesman may stop play and impose any major penalty when a serious incident has occurred.

The Linesman must report upon completion of play, any circumstances pertaining to:.

1. Match penalties: Rule 43 – Attempt to Injure and Rule 52 – Deliberate Injury of Opponents.
2. Bench minor penalties (Unsportsmanlike Conduct): Rule 41(a) – Abuse of Officials.
3. Misconducts, Game Misconducts and Gross Misconducts: Rule 28 – Misconduct Penalties.
4. Interference with a goalkeeper when a goal has been scored.

(b) The Linesman shall face-off the puck at all times except to start the game. When the two referee system is in use, the Linesman shall face-off the puck at all times except at the start of each period and following the scoring of a goal.

(c) The Linesman shall give to the Referee his interpretation of any incident that may have taken place during the game.

Rule 37. Goal Judge

(a) There shall be one Goal Judge at each goal. They shall not be members of either club engaged in a game, nor shall they be replaced during its progress, unless after the commencement of the game it becomes apparent that either Goal Judge, on account of partisanship or any other cause, is guilty of giving unjust decisions, when the Referee may appoint another Goal Judge to act in his stead.

(b) Goal Judges shall be stationed behind the goals during the progress of play, in properly protected areas, if possible, so that there can be no interference with their activities. They shall not change goals during the game.

(c) In the event of a goal being claimed, the Goal Judge of that goal shall decide whether or not the puck has passed between the goal posts and entirely over the goal line.

Rule 38. Penalty Timekeeper

(a) The Penalty Timekeeper shall keep, on the official forms provided, a correct record of all penalties imposed by the Officials including the names of the players penalized, the infractions penalized, the duration of each penalty and the time at which each penalty was imposed. He shall report in the Penalty Record each penalty shot awarded, the name of the player taking the shot and the result of the shot. He shall also record in the Penalty

---

Record the details and the result of any stick measurement performed by the Referee during the game.

(b) The Penalty Timekeeper shall check and ensure that the time served by all penalized players is correct. He shall be responsible for the correct posting of penalties on the scoreboard at all times and shall promptly call to the attention of the Referee any discrepancy between the time recorded on the clock and the official correct time and he shall be responsible for making any adjustments ordered by the Referee.

He shall upon request, give a penalized player correct information as to the unexpired time of his penalty.

(NOTE 1) The infraction of the rules for which each penalty has been imposed will be announced twice over the public address system as reported by the Referee. Where players of both Teams are penalized on the same play, the penalty to the visiting player will be announced first.

(NOTE 2) Misconduct penalties and coincident major penalties should not be recorded on the timing device but such penalized players should be alerted and released at the first stoppage of play following the expiration of their penalties.

(c) Upon the completion of each game, the Penalty Timekeeper shall complete and sign four copies of the Penalty Record to be distributed as quickly as possible to the following persons:

(1) One copy to the Official Scorer for

transmission to the League
Commissioner;

(2) One copy to the visiting Coach or Manager;

(3) One copy to the home Coach or Manager;

(4) One copy to the home Team Public
Relations Department.

(d) The Officiating Department shall be entitled to inspect, collect and forward to League head-quarters the actual work sheets used by the Penalty Timekeeper in any game.

(e) The Penalty Timekeeper shall have an official stick measuring gauge available for the Officials' use during the game.

Rule 39. Official Scorer

(a) Before the start of the game, the Official Scorer shall obtain from the Manager or Coach of both Teams a list of all eligible players and the starting line-up of each Team which information shall be made known to the opposing Manager or Coach before the start of play, either personally or through the Referee.

The Official Scorer shall secure the names of the Captain and Alternate Captains from the Manager or Coach at the time the line-ups are collected and will indicate those nominated by placing the letter "C" or "A" opposite their names on the Referee's Report of Match. All this information shall be presented to the Referee for his signature at the completion of the game.

(b) The Official Scorer shall keep a record of the goals scored, the scorers, and players to whom assists have been credited and shall indicate those players on the lists who have actually taken part in the game. He shall also record the time of entry into the game of any substitute goalkeeper. He shall record on the Official Score Sheet a notation where a goal is scored when the goalkeeper has been removed from the ice.

(c) The Official Scorer shall award the points for goals and assists and his decision shall be final. The Official Scorer shall use the Video Goal Judge system to verify the proper awarding of goals and assists. The awards of points for goals and assists shall be announced twice over the public address system and all changes in such awards shall also be announced in the same manner.

No requests for changes in any award of points shall be considered unless they are made at or before the conclusion of actual play in the game by the Team Captain.

(d) At the conclusion of the game, the Official Scorer shall complete and sign four copies of the Official Score Sheet for distribution as quickly as possible to the following persons:

(1) One copy to the Official Scorer to be transmitted to the League Commissioner;

(2) One copy to the visiting Coach or Manager;

(3) One copy to the home Coach or Manager;

(4)   One copy to the home Team Public
Relations Department.

(e) The Official Scorer shall also prepare the
Official Report of Match for signature by the
Referee and forward it to the League
Commissioner together with the Official Score
Sheet and the Penalty Record.

(f) The Official Scorer should be in an elevated
position, well away from the players' benches,
with house telephone communication to the
public address announcer.

Rule 40. Game Timekeeper

(a) The Game Timekeeper shall record the time of
starting and finishing of each period in the
game. During the game the Game Timekeeper
will start the clock with the drop of the puck
and stop the clock upon hearing the Officials'
whistle or the scoring of a goal.

Any loss of time on the game or penalty
clocks due to a false face-off must be replaced.
The Video Goal Judge may be consulted to
ensure the time is accurately replaced.

(b) The Game Timekeeper shall signal the Referee
and the competing Teams for the start of the
game and each succeeding period and the
Referee shall start the play promptly in
accordance with Rule 90 – Time of Match.

For the purpose of keeping the spectators
informed as to the time remaining during
intermissions, the Game Timekeeper will use
the electric clock to record the length of

intermissions. The clock will not start for the intermission until all players and Officials have left the ice.

To assist in assuring the prompt return to the ice of the Teams and the Officials, the Game Timekeeper shall give preliminary warnings five (5) and two (2) minutes prior to the resumption of play in each period.

(c) If the rink is not equipped with an automatic signalling device or, if such device fails to function, the Game Timekeeper shall signal the end of each period by blowing a whistle.

(d) He shall cause to be announced on the public address system at the nineteenth minute in each period that there is one minute remaining to be played in the period.

(e) In the event of any dispute regarding time, the matter shall be referred to the Referee for adjustment and his decision shall be final. The Game Timekeeper shall assist to verify game time via an additional timing device. (NHL approved stop watch)

(f) The Game Timekeeper is required to synchronize his timing device with the Television Producer of the originating broadcast.

(g) In accordance with Rule 93 – Video Goal Judge, the Officials may use the Video Goal Judge system to establish the correct time on the official game clock, provided the game time is visible on the Video Goal Judge's monitors.

Rule 40A. Statistician

(a) There shall be appointed for duty at every game played in the League a Statistician and such assistants or alternates as may be deemed necessary.

(b) The duty of the Statistician(s) is to correctly record on official League forms all of the required data concerning the performances of the individual players and Teams.

(c) These records shall be compiled and recorded in strict conformity with the instructions printed on the forms supplied and shall be completed as to totals where required and with such accuracy as to ensure that the data supplied is "in balance".

(d) At the conclusion of each game, the Statistician shall sign and distribute four copies of the final and correct Statistician's Report to each of the following persons:

  (1) One copy to the Official Scorer for transmission to the League Commissioner;

  (2) One copy to the visiting Coach or Manager;

  (3) One copy to the home Coach or Manager;

  (4) One copy to the home Team Public Relations Department.

SECTION SIX – PLAYING RULES

Rule 41. Abuse of Officials and other Misconduct

(NOTE) In the enforcement of this Rule, the Referee has, in many instances, the option of imposing a misconduct penalty or a bench minor penalty. In principle, the Referee is directed to impose a bench minor penalty in respect to the violations which occur on or in the immediate vicinity of the players' bench but off the playing surface and in all cases affecting non-playing personnel or players. A misconduct penalty should be imposed for violations which occur on the playing surface or in the penalty bench area and where the penalized player is readily identifiable.

(a) A misconduct penalty shall be imposed on any player who uses obscene, profane or abusive language to any person or who intentionally knocks or shoots the puck out of the reach of an Official who is retrieving it or who deliberately throws any equipment out of the playing area.

(b) A minor penalty shall be assessed to any player who challenges or disputes the rulings of any Official during a game. If the player persists in such challenge or dispute, he shall be assessed a misconduct penalty and any further

UNSPORTSMANLIKE CONDUCT
Use both hands to form a "T" in front of the chest.

dispute will result in a game misconduct penalty being assessed to the offending player.

In the event that a teammate of a penalized player challenges or disputes the ruling of the Official in assessing the penalty, a misconduct penalty shall be imposed.

(NOTE) Any player who, having entered the penalty bench, leaves the penalty bench prior to the expiration of his penalty, shall be assessed the appropriate penalties. He shall also be automatically suspended for the next three regular League and/or playoff games of his club. This Rule does not replace any other more severe penalty that may be imposed for leaving the penalty bench. See also Rule 72 – Leaving Players' or Penalty Bench.

(c) A misconduct penalty shall be imposed on any player or players who bang the boards with their sticks or other objects at any time, showing disrespect for an Official's decision.

In the event that the Coach, Trainer, Manager or club executive commits an infraction under this Rule, a bench minor penalty shall be imposed.

(d) Where coincident penalties are imposed on players of both Teams, the penalized players of the visiting Team shall take their positions on the penalty bench first in the place designated for visiting players.

(e) Any player who, following a fight or other altercation in which he has been involved is broken up and for which he is penalized, fails to proceed directly and immediately to the penalty bench, or who causes any delay by retrieving his equipment (gloves, sticks, etc. shall be delivered to him at the penalty bench by teammates), shall incur an automatic fine of one hundred dollars ($100) in addition to all other penalties or fines incurred.

(f) Any player who persists in continuing or attempting to continue a fight or altercation after he has been ordered by the Referee to stop, or who resists a Linesman in the discharge of his duties shall, at the discretion of the Referee, incur a misconduct or game misconduct penalty in addition to any penalties imposed. (See also Rule 76 – Physical Abuse of Officials.)

(g) A misconduct penalty shall be imposed on any player who, after warning by the Referee, persists in any course of conduct (including threatening or abusive language or gestures or similar actions) designed to incite an opponent into incurring a penalty.

If, after the assessment of a misconduct penalty, a player persists in any course of conduct for which he was previously assessed a misconduct penalty, he shall be assessed a game misconduct penalty.

(h) A bench minor penalty shall be imposed against the offending Team if any player, club executive, Manager, Coach or Trainer uses obscene, profane or abusive language or gesture to any person or uses the name of any

Official coupled with any vociferous remarks.

(i) In the case of any club executive, Manager, Coach or Trainer being guilty of such misconduct, he is to be removed from the bench by order of the Referee and his case reported to the Commissioner for further action. (Refer to Rule 73(c) – Obscene or Profane Language or Gestures.)

(j) If any club executive, Manager, Coach or Trainer is removed from the bench by order of the Referee, he must not sit near the bench of his club nor in any way direct or attempt to direct the play of his club.

When a Coach has been removed from the bench, he shall be assessed a game misconduct penalty.

(k) A bench minor penalty shall be imposed against the offending Team if any player, Trainer, Coach, Manager or club executive in the vicinity of the players' bench or penalty bench throws anything on the ice during the progress of the game or during stoppage of play.

> *(NOTE) The penalty provided under this Rule is in addition to any penalty imposed under Rule 45(c) – Broken Stick.*

(l) A bench minor penalty shall be imposed against the offending Team if any player, Trainer, Coach, Manager or club executive interferes in any manner with any game official including the Referee, Linesmen, Timekeepers or Goal Judges in the performance of their duties.

The Referee may assess further penalties under Rule 76 (Abuse of Officials) if he deems them to be warranted.

(m) A misconduct penalty shall be imposed on any player or players who, except for the purpose of taking their positions on the penalty bench, enter or remain in the Referee's crease while he is reporting to or consulting with any game official including Linesmen, Timekeeper, Penalty Timekeeper, Official Scorer or Announcer.

(n) A minor penalty shall be imposed on any player who is guilty of unsportsmanlike conduct including, but not limited to hair-pulling, biting, grabbing hold of face mask, etc.

(NOTE) If warranted the Referee may apply Rule 28(d) – Gross Misconduct.

(o) A minor penalty shall be imposed on a player who attempts to draw a penalty by his actions ("diving").

Rule 42. Adjustment to Clothing or Equipment

(a) Play shall not be stopped nor the game delayed by reasons of adjustments to clothing, equipment, skates or sticks.

For an infringement of this Rule, a minor penalty shall be given.

(b) The onus of maintaining clothing and equipment in proper condition shall be upon the player. If adjustments are required, the

player shall leave the ice and play shall
continue with a substitute.

(c) No delay shall be permitted for the repair or
adjustment of goalkeeper's equipment. If
adjustments are required, the goalkeeper shall
leave the ice and his place shall be taken by
the substitute goalkeeper immediately.

(d) For an infraction of this Rule by a goalkeeper,
a minor penalty shall be imposed.

Rule 43. Attempt to Injure

(a) A match penalty shall be imposed on any
player who deliberately attempts to injure an
opponent and the circumstances shall be
reported to the Commissioner for further
action. A substitute for the penalized player
shall be permitted at the end of the fifth
minute.

(b) A game misconduct penalty shall be imposed
on any player who deliberately attempts to
injure an Official, Manager, Coach or Trainer
in any manner and the circumstances shall be
reported to the Commissioner for further
action. (See also Rule 76 – Physical Abuse of
Officials.)

> *(NOTE) The Commissioner, upon preliminary
> investigation indicating the probable imposition of
> supplementary disciplinary action, may order the
> immediate suspension of a player who has
> incurred a match penalty under this Rule, pending
> the final determination of such supplementary
> disciplinary action.*

Rule 44. Boarding

(a) A minor or major penalty, at the discretion of the Referee, based upon the degree of violence of the impact with the boards, shall be imposed on any player who checks an opponent in such a manner that causes the opponent to be thrown violently in the boards.

BOARDING
Pounding the closed fist of one hand into the open palm of the other hand.

(NOTE) Any unnecessary contact with a player playing the puck on an obvious "icing" or "off-side" play which results in that player being knocked into the boards is "boarding" and must be penalized as such. In other instances where there is no contact with the boards, it should be treated as "charging".

(b) When a major penalty is imposed under this Rule for a foul resulting in an injury to the face or head of an opponent, a game misconduct shall be imposed.

(c) Any player who incurs a total of two (2) game misconducts for Boarding under Rule 44 (b), in either Regular Season or Playoffs, shall be suspended automatically for the next game of his Team. For each subsequent game misconduct penalty the automatic suspension shall be increased by one game.

(d) When a major penalty is imposed under this Rule, an automatic fine of one hundred dollars ($100) shall be imposed.

Rule 45. Broken Stick

(NOTE) A broken stick is one which, in the opinion of the Referee, is unfit for normal play.

(a) A player without a stick may participate in the game. A player whose stick is broken may participate in the game provided he drops the broken stick. A minor penalty shall be imposed for an infraction of this Rule.

(b) A goalkeeper may continue to play with a broken stick until a stoppage of play or until he has been legally provided with a stick.

NEW

(c) A player who has lost or broken his stick may only receive a stick at his own players' bench or be handed one from a teammate on the ice. A minor penalty shall be imposed for an infraction of this Rule.

(NOTE) A player tendered a stick thrown on the ice from the players' or penalty bench will not receive a penalty. However, the person responsible for throwing the stick will receive the penalty, as covered in Rule 41(k) – Abuse of Officials and Other Misconduct and Rule 67(g)(h)(i) – Interference.

(d) A goalkeeper whose stick is broken or illegal may not go to the players' bench for a replacement but must receive his stick from a teammate.

For an infraction of this Rule, a minor penalty shall be imposed on the goalkeeper.

Rule 46. Butt-Ending

(NOTE) Butt-ending shall mean using the end of the shaft of the stick in a jabbing motion.

(a) A double-minor penalty will be imposed on a player who attempts to butt-end an opponent.

(b) A major penalty and a game misconduct shall be imposed on a player who butt-ends an opponent. See also Rule 43 – Attempt to Injure.

   In addition to the major penalty and game misconduct imposed under this Rule, an automatic fine of one hundred dollars ($100) will be imposed.

(c) A match penalty shall be imposed on a player who injures an opponent as a result of a butt-end. See also Rule 52 – Deliberate Injury of Opponents.

Rule 47. Charging

Charging shall mean the actions of a player who, as a result of distance traveled, shall violently check an opponent in any manner. A "Charge" may be the result of a check into the boards, into the goal frame or in open ice.

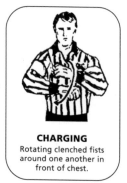

CHARGING
Rotating clenched fists around one another in front of chest.

(a) A minor or major penalty shall be imposed on a player who skates or jumps into, or charges an opponent in any manner.

(b) When a major penalty is imposed under this

Rule for a foul resulting in an injury to the face or head of an opponent, a game misconduct shall be imposed, and an automatic fine of one hundred dollars ($100).

(c) A minor, major or a major and a game misconduct shall be imposed on a player who charges a goalkeeper while the goalkeeper is within his goal crease.

(NOTE) A goalkeeper is NOT "fair game" just because he is outside the goal crease area. The appropriate penalty should be assessed in every case where an opposing player makes unnecessary contact with a goalkeeper. However, incidental contact, at the discretion of the Referee, will be permitted when the goalkeeper is in the act of playing the puck outside his goal crease provided the attacking player has made a reasonable effort to avoid such contact.

Although goalkeepers are provided with additional protection under Rule 78 – Protection of the Goalkeeper, they are still subject to penalties for infractions of the rules that they commit in or out of the goal crease. Particular attention will be made by the Referees to goalkeepers that embellish the contact in an attempt to draw a penalty.

Rule 48. Checking from Behind

A check from behind is a check delivered on a player who is not aware of the impending hit, therefore UNABLE TO DEFEND HIMSELF, and contact is made on the back part of the body. When a player intentionally turns his body to create contact with his back, no penalty shall be assessed

(a) Any player who cross-checks, pushes or charges from behind an opponent who is unable to defend himself, shall be assessed a major and a game misconduct. This penalty applies anywhere on the playing surface.

(b) Any player who incurs a total of two (2) game misconducts for Checking from Behind under Rule 48(a) in either Regular Season or Playoffs, shall be suspended automatically for the next game of his Team. For each subsequent game misconduct penalty the automatic suspension shall be increased by one game.

Rule 49. Clipping

Clipping is the act of throwing the body, from any direction, across or below the knees of an opponent.

(a) A player may not deliver a check in a "clipping" manner, nor lower his own body position to deliver a check on or below an opponent's knees.

(b) An illegal "low hit" is a check that is delivered by a player who may or may not have both skates on the ice, with his sole intent to check the opponent in the area of his knees. A player may not lower his body position to deliver a check to an opponent's knees.

A player who commits these fouls will be assessed a minor penalty for "clipping". If an injury occurs as a result of this "clipping" check, the player must be assessed a major and a game misconduct.

Rule 50. Cross-Checking

(NOTE) A cross-check shall mean a check rendered with both hands on the stick, and the extending of the arms, while the check is being delivered.

(a) A minor or major penalty, at the discretion of the Referee, shall be imposed on a player who "cross-checks" an opponent.

When a major penalty is assessed for cross-checking, an automatic game misconduct penalty shall be imposed on the offending player.

CROSS-CHECKING
A forward and backward motion with both fists clenched extending from the chest.

(b) When a major penalty is imposed under this Rule, an automatic fine of one hundred dollars ($100) shall also be imposed.

Rule 51. Delaying the Game

(a) A minor penalty shall be imposed on any player or goalkeeper who delays the game by deliberately shooting or batting the puck with his stick outside the playing area.

> *(NOTE 1) When the goalkeeper shoots the puck directly (non-deflected) out of the playing surface, except where there is no glass, a penalty shall be assessed for delaying the game.*

> *(NOTE 2) This penalty shall also apply when a player or goalkeeper deliberately bats or shoots the puck with his stick outside the playing area after a stoppage of play.*

(b) A minor penalty shall be imposed on any player or goalkeeper who throws or deliberately bats the puck with his hand or stick outside the playing area.

(c) A minor penalty shall be imposed on any player (including the goalkeeper) who delays the game by deliberately displacing a goal post from its normal position. The Referee or Linesmen shall stop play immediately when the offending Team gains possession of the puck.

If the goal post is deliberately displaced by a goalkeeper or player during the course of a "breakaway", a penalty shot will be awarded to the non-offending Team, which shot shall be taken by the player last in possession of the puck.

(NOTE) A player with a "breakaway" is defined as a player in control of the puck with no opposition between him and the opposing goal and with a reasonable scoring opportunity.

In the event that a goalpost is deliberately displaced by a defending player or goalkeeper, prior to the puck crossing the goal line between the normal position of the goalposts, the Referee, at his discretion, may assess a minor penalty under Rule 51(c) (paragraph 1), a penalty shot under Rule 51(d), or award a goal.

(d) If by reason of insufficient time in the regular playing time or by reason of penalties already imposed, the minor penalty assessed to a player for deliberately displacing his own goal post cannot be served in its entirety within the regular playing time of the game or at any time in overtime, a penalty shot shall be awarded against the offending Team.

(e) A bench minor penalty shall be imposed upon any Team which, after warning by the Referee to its Captain or Alternate Captain to place the correct number of players on the ice and commence play, fails to comply with the Referee's direction and thereby causes any delay by making additional substitutions, by persisting in having its players off-side, or in any other manner.

Rule 52. Deliberate Injury of Opponents

(a) A match penalty shall be imposed on a player who deliberately injures an opponent in any manner.

> *(NOTE) Any player wearing tape or any other material on his hands (below the wrist) who cuts or injures an opponent during an altercation shall receive a match penalty under this Rule.*

(b) In addition to the match penalty, the player shall be automatically suspended from further competition until the Commissioner has ruled on the issue.

(c) No substitute shall be permitted to take the place of the penalized player until five (5) minutes of actual playing time have elapsed from the time the penalty was imposed.

(d) A game misconduct penalty shall be imposed on any player who deliberately injures an Official, Manager, Coach or Trainer in any manner and the circumstances shall be reported to the Commissioner for further action.

Rule 53. Elbowing

Elbowing shall mean the use of an extended elbow in a manner that may or may not cause injury.

ELBOWING
Tapping the elbow of the "whistle hand" with the opposite hand.

(a) A minor or major penalty, at the discretion of the Referee, shall be imposed on any player who uses his elbow to foul an opponent.

(b) When a major penalty is imposed under this Rule for a foul resulting in an injury to the face or head of an opponent, a game misconduct shall be imposed and an automatic fine of one hundred dollars ($100).

Rule 54. Face-Offs

Conduct of any face-off commences when the Official designates the place of the face-off and he takes up his position to drop the puck.

(a) The puck shall be faced-off by the Referee or the Linesman dropping the puck on the ice between the sticks of the players facing-off. Players facing-off will stand squarely facing their opponent's end of the rink approximately one stick length apart with the blade of their sticks on the ice.

When the face-off takes place in any of the end face-off circles, the players taking part shall take their position so that they will stand squarely facing their opponent's end of the rink, and clear of the ice markings. The sticks of both players facing-off shall have the blade on the ice, within the designated white area. The visiting player shall place his stick within the designated white area first followed IMMEDIATELY by the home player.

No other player shall be allowed to enter the face-off circle or come within fifteen feet (15') of the players facing-off. All players must stand on side on all face-offs.

If a violation of this sub-section occurs, the Referee or Linesman shall conduct the face-off again.

(b) If after warning by the Referee or Linesman, either of the players fails to take his proper position for the face-off promptly, the Official shall be entitled to face-off the puck notwithstanding such default.

(c) In the conduct of any face-off anywhere on the playing surface, no player facing-off shall make any physical contact with his opponent's body by means of his own body or by his stick except in the course of playing the puck after the face-off has been completed.

For violation of this Rule, the Referee shall impose a minor penalty or penalties on the player(s) whose action(s) caused the physical contact.

(d) If a player facing-off fails to take his proper position immediately when directed by the

Official, the Official may order him replaced for that face-off by any teammate then on the ice.

No substitution of players shall be permitted until the face-off has been completed and play has resumed except when a penalty is imposed which affects the on-ice strength of either Team.

(e) A second violation of any of the provisions of sub-section (a) hereof by the same Team during the same face-off shall be penalized with a minor penalty to the player who commits the second violation of the Rule. The Official must drop the puck twice in order to have a second face-off violation. Any loss of time on the game or penalty clocks must be replaced. the Video Goal Judge may be consulted to ensure the time is accurately replaced.

During end zone face-offs, all other players on the ice must position their bodies on their own side of the restraining lines marked on the outer edge of the face-off circles.

If a player other than the player taking the face-off moves into the face-off circle prior to the dropping of the puck, then the offending Team's player taking the face-off shall be ejected from the face-off circle.

If a violation of this Rule occurs, the Referee or Linesman shall order another face-off, unless the non-offending Team wins the draw and retains possession of the puck.

(f) When an infringement of a rule has been committed or a stoppage of play has been caused by any player of the attacking side in the attacking zone, the ensuing face-off shall be made in the neutral zone on the nearest face-off spot.

(g) When an infringement of a rule has been committed by players of both sides in the play resulting in the stoppage, the ensuing face-off will be made at the place of such infringement or at the place where play is stopped.

(h) When stoppage occurs between the end face-off spots and near end of the rink, the puck shall be faced-off at the end face-off spot on the side where the stoppage occurs unless otherwise expressly provided by these Rules.

(i) No face-off shall be made within fifteen feet (15')of the goal or sideboards.

(j) When a goal is illegally scored as a result of a puck being deflected directly off an Official anywhere in the defending zone, the resulting face-off shall be made at the end face-off spot in the defending zone.

(k) When the game is stopped for any reason not specifically covered in the Official Rules, the puck must be faced-off where it was last played.

(l) The whistle will not be blown by the Official to start play. Playing time will commence from the instant the puck is faced-off and will stop when the whistle is blown or a goal is scored.

(m) Following a stoppage of play, should one or both defensemen who are the point players or any player coming from the bench of the attacking Team, enter into the attacking zone beyond the outer edge of the end zone face-off circle during an altercation or "scrum," the ensuing face-off shall take place in the neutral zone near the blue line of the defending Team.

Rule 55. Falling on Puck

(a) A minor penalty shall be imposed on a player other than the goalkeeper who deliberately falls on or gathers the puck into his body.

> *(NOTE) Any player who drops to his knees to block a shot should not be penalized if the puck is shot under him or becomes lodged in his clothing or equipment but any use of the hands to make the puck unplayable should be penalized promptly.*

(b) A minor penalty shall be imposed on a goalkeeper who, when he is in his own goal crease, deliberately falls on or gathers the puck into his body or who holds or places the puck against any part of the goal in such a manner as to cause a stoppage of play unless he is actually being checked by an opponent.

> *(NOTE) Refer to Rule 79(b) – Puck Must Be Kept In Motion for the Rule governing freezing of the puck by a goalkeeper outside of his crease area.*

(c) No defending player, except the goalkeeper, will be permitted to fall on the puck, hold the puck or gather the puck into the body or hands when the puck is within the goal crease.

For infringement of this Rule, play shall

---

immediately be stopped and a penalty shot shall be ordered against the offending Team, but no other penalty shall be given.

(NOTE) The Rule shall be interpreted so that a penalty shot will be awarded only when the puck is in the crease at the instant the offense occurs. However, in cases where the puck is outside the crease, Rule 55(a) may still apply and a minor penalty may be imposed, even though no penalty shot is awarded.

Rule 56. Fisticuffs

An instigator of an altercation shall be a player who by his actions or demeanor demonstrates any/some of the following criteria: distance traveled; gloves off first; first punch thrown; menacing attitude or posture; verbal instigation or threats; conduct in retaliation to a prior game incident.

An altercation is a situation involving two players, with at least one to be penalized.

(a) A minor (roughing), major or a major and a game misconduct, at the discretion of the Referee, shall be imposed on any player involved in fisticuffs.

A player who is deemed to be the instigator of an altercation shall be assessed an instigating minor penalty, a major for fighting and a ten minute misconduct.

A player who is assessed a major and a game misconduct for being an instigator/aggressor of an altercation will have this recorded as an instigator of an altercation for statistical and suspension purposes.

If the same player is deemed to be the instigator of a second altercation in the same game, he shall be assessed an instigating minor penalty, a major for fighting and a game misconduct.

A player who is deemed to be the instigator of an altercation for the third time in one Regular Season shall be assessed a minor penalty (instigating), a major (fighting) and a game misconduct. He subsequently shall be suspended for the next two Regular Season games of his Team. For the fourth instigator penalty in the same Regular Season, the player will be suspended for the next four games of his Team. For the fifth instigator penalty in the same Regular Season, the player will be suspended for the next six games of his Team.

If a player penalized as an instigator of an altercation is wearing a face shield, he shall be assessed an additional Unsportsmanlike Conduct penalty.

NEW

A player who deliberately removes his sweater prior to participating in an altercation or who is clearly wearing a sweater that has been modified and does not conform to Rule 24A – Players' Jerseys, shall be assessed a minor penalty for Unsportsmanlike Conduct and a game misconduct. This is in addition to other penalties to be assessed to the participants of an altercation.

A player who engages in fisticuffs and whose sweater is removed (completely off his

---

torso), other than through the actions of his opponent in the altercation or through the actions of the Linesman, shall be assessed a game misconduct penalty.

A player who engages in fisticuffs and whose sweater is not properly "tied-down" (sweater properly fastened to pants), and who loses his sweater (completely off his torso) in that altercation, shall receive a game misconduct.

A player who is involved in an altercation, when the opponent has been identified as an instigator, shall not be assessed a game misconduct if his sweater should be removed by an opponent or an Official in the discharge of his duties.

(b) A minor penalty shall be imposed on a player who, having been struck, shall retaliate with a blow or attempted blow. However, at the discretion of the Referee, a major or a double-minor penalty or a game misconduct penalty may be imposed if such player continues the altercation.

> *(NOTE 1) It is the intent and purpose of this Rule that the Referee shall impose the "major and game misconduct" penalty in all cases where the instigator or retaliator of the fight is the aggressor and is plainly doing so for the purpose of intimidation or punishment.*

> *(NOTE 2) The Referee is provided very wide latitude in the penalties which he may impose under this Rule. This is done intentionally to enable him to differentiate between the obvious degrees of*

*responsibility of the participants either for starting
the fighting or persisting in continuing the fighting.
The discretion provided should be exercised
realistically.*

*(NOTE 3) Referees are directed to employ every
means provided by these rules to stop "brawling" and
should use this Rule and Rules 41(e) and (f) – Abuse
of Officials and other Misconduct.*

*(NOTE 4) Any player wearing tape or any other
material on his hands (below the wrist) who cuts or
injures an opponent during an altercation will
receive a match penalty under Rule 52 – Deliberate
Injury of Opponents.*

(c) A misconduct or game misconduct penalty
shall be imposed on any player involved in
fisticuffs off the playing surface or with
another player who is off the playing surface.
These penalties are in addition to any other
time penalties assessed.

(d) A game misconduct penalty, at the discretion of
the Referee, shall be imposed on any player or
goalkeeper who is the first to intervene in an
altercation already in progress except when a
match penalty is being imposed in the original
altercation. This penalty is in addition to any
other penalty incurred in the same incident.

(e) When a fight occurs, all players not engaged
shall go immediately to the area of their
players' bench and in the event the altercation
takes place at a players' bench, the players on
the ice from that Team shall go to their
defensive zone.

Failure to comply with the Rule shall, in
addition to the other penalties that may be

assessed, result in a fine to the Team of $1,000 and the Coach of said Team in the amount of $1,000.

(f) A game misconduct penalty shall be imposed on any player who is assessed a major penalty for fighting after the original altercation.

Notwithstanding this Rule, at the discretion of the Referee, the automatic game misconduct penalty may be waived for a player in the altercation if the opposing player was clearly the instigator of the altercation.

(g) Any Teams whose players become involved in an altercation, other than during the periods of the game, shall be fined automatically twenty-five thousand dollars ($25,000) in addition to any other appropriate penalties that may be imposed upon the participating players by supplementary discipline or otherwise.

Any player who would be deemed to be an instigator pursuant to Rule 56(a) at a time other than during the periods of the game shall be suspended automatically for ten (10) games. Such determination may be made by the Referee at the time of the incident or subsequently by the Commissioner or his designee based upon such reports and other information as he deems sufficient, including but not limited to television tapes.

(NOTE) In the case of altercations taking place after the period or game the fine under this Rule shall be assessed only in the event that an altercation is commenced after the period or game has terminated.

Rule 57. Goals and Assists

(NOTE) It is the responsibility of the Official Scorer to award goals and assists, and his decision in this respect is final, notwithstanding the report of the Referee or any other game Official. The use of Video Replay to verify the proper awarding of a goal or an assist is essential. Such awards shall be made or withheld strictly in accordance with the provisions of this Rule. Therefore, it is essential that the Official Scorer be thoroughly familiar with every aspect of this Rule; be alert to observe all actions which could affect the awarding of a goal or assist; and, above all, give or withhold awards with absolute impartiality.

In case of an obvious error in awarding a goal or an assist that has been announced, it should be corrected promptly, but changes should not be made in the Official Scoring Summary after the Referee has signed the Game Report.

(a) A goal shall be scored when the puck shall have been put between the goal posts by the stick of a player of the attacking side, from in front and below the crossbar, and entirely across a red line the width of the diameter of the goal posts drawn on the ice from one goal post to the other with the goal frame in its proper position. (See also Rule 51(c) – Delaying the Game.)

(b) A goal shall be scored if the puck is put into the goal in any way by a player of the defending side. The player of the attacking side who last played the puck shall be credited with the goal but no assist shall be awarded.

(c) A goal cannot be scored by an attacking player

who deliberately bats the puck with any part of his body across the goal line. A goal cannot be scored where an attacking player bats the puck and it is deflected off any player or goalkeeper into the net.

(d) If an attacking player has the puck deflect into the net, off his skate or body, in any manner, the goal shall be allowed. The player who deflected the puck shall be credited with the goal.

WASH-OUT
Both arms swung laterally across the body with palms down. When used by the Referee, it means goal disallowed.

The goal shall not be allowed if the puck has been intentionally kicked with his skate or foot, using a distinct kicking motion, and subsequently enters the net.

A goal shall be allowed unless a distinct kicking motion is evident.

The goal shall not be allowed if the puck has been thrown or otherwise deliberately directed into the goal by any means other than a stick. (See also Rule 70 – Kicking the Puck.)

(e) If a goal is scored as a result of being deflected directly into the net off an Official, the goal

shall not be allowed. Refer to Rule 82 – Puck
Striking Official.

(f) Should a player legally propel a puck into the
goal crease of the opponent club and the puck
should become loose and available to another
player of the attacking side, a goal scored on
the play shall be legal.

(g) Any goal scored, other than as covered by the
Official Rules, shall not be allowed.

(h) A "goal" shall be credited in the scoring records
to a player who shall have propelled the puck
into the opponent's goal. Each "goal" shall
count one point in the player's record.

(i) When a player scores a goal, an "assist" shall be
credited to the player or players taking part in
the play immediately preceding the goal, but
no more than two assists can be given on any
goal. Each "assist" shall count one point in the
player's record.

(j) Only one point can be credited to any one
player on a goal.

Rule 58. Gross Misconduct

The Referee may impose a "GROSS
MISCONDUCT" penalty on any player,
Manager, Coach or Trainer who is guilty of
gross misconduct of any kind. Any person
incurring a "gross misconduct" penalty shall be
suspended for the balance of the game and
shall incur an automatic fine of two hundred
dollars ($200) and the case shall be referred to

the Commissioner of the League for further
disciplinary action. (See also Rule 28(d) –
Misconduct Penalties.)

*(NOTE) For all game misconduct and gross mis-
conduct penalties regardless of when imposed, a
total of ten minutes shall be charged in the records
against the offending player.*

Rule 59. Handling Puck with Hands

(a) If a player, except a goalkeeper, closes his
hand on the puck, the play shall be stopped
and a minor penalty shall be imposed on him. A
goalkeeper who holds the puck with his hands
for longer than three seconds shall be given a
minor penalty unless he is actually being
checked by an opponent.

(b) A goalkeeper must not deliberately hold the
puck in any manner which, in the opinion of
the Referee, causes a stoppage of play, nor
throw the puck forward towards the opponent's
net, nor deliberately drop the puck into his
pads or onto the goal net, nor deliberately pile
up snow or obstacles at or near his net, that in
the opinion of the Referee, would tend to
prevent the scoring of a goal.

*(NOTE) The object of this entire Rule is to keep the
puck in play continuously and any action taken
by the goalkeeper which causes an unnecessary
stoppage must be penalized without warning.*

(c) The penalty for infringement of this Rule by
the goalkeeper shall be a minor penalty.

*(NOTE) In the case where the puck thrown forward
by the goalkeeper being taken by an opponent, the*

> *Referee shall allow the resulting play to be completed, and if goal is scored by the non-offending Team, it shall be allowed and no penalty given; but if a goal is not scored, play shall be stopped and a minor penalty shall be imposed against the goalkeeper.*

(d) A minor penalty shall be imposed on a player, except the goalkeeper, who, while play is in progress, picks up the puck off the ice with his hand.

If a player, except a goalkeeper, while play is in progress, picks up the puck with his hand from the ice in the goal crease area, the play shall be stopped immediately and a penalty shot shall be awarded to the non-offending Team.

(e) A player shall be permitted to stop or "bat" a puck in the air with his open hand, or push it along the ice with his hand, and the play shall not be stopped unless, in the opinion of the Referee, he has deliberately directed the puck to a teammate in any zone other than the defensive zone, in which case the play shall be stopped and the puck faced-off at the spot where the offense occurred. Play will not be stopped for any hand pass by players in their own defensive zone.

> *(NOTE) The object of this Rule is to ensure continuous action and the Referee should NOT stop play unless he is satisfied that the directing of the puck to a teammate was, in fact, DELIBERATE.*

A goal cannot be scored by an attacking

player who bats the puck with his hand directly into the net. A goal cannot be scored by an attacking player who bats the puck and it is deflected into the net off any player or goalkeeper.

Rule 60. Head-Butting

(a) A double minor penalty shall be imposed on a player who attempts to head-butt an opponent.

(b) A major and a game misconduct penalty shall be imposed on a player who head-butts an opponent. (See also Rule 43 – Attempt to Injure.)

(c) A match penalty shall be imposed on a player who injures an opponent as a result of a head-butt. (See also Rule 52 – Deliberate Injury of Opponent.)

Rule 61. High Sticks

A "high stick" is one which is carried above the height of the opponent's shoulders. A player is permitted accidental contact on an opponent if the act is committed as a normal windup or follow through of a shooting motion.

HIGH-STICKING
Holding both fists, clenched, one above the other at the side of the head.

(a) Any contact made by a stick on an opponent above the shoulders is prohibited and a minor shall be imposed subject to section (b) of this Rule.

(b) When a player carries or holds any part of his stick above the shoulders of the opponent so that injury results, the Referee shall:

  (i) Assess a double minor penalty for all contact that causes an injury, whether accidental or careless, in the opinion of the Referee.

  (ii) Assess a match penalty to a player, who in the opinion of the Referee attempted to injure an opponent. (See Rule 43 – Attempt to Injure.)

  (iii) Assess a match penalty to a player, who in the opinion of the Referee deliberately injured an opponent. (See Rule 52 – Deliberate Injury of Opponents.)

(c) An apparent goal scored by an attacking player who strikes the puck with his stick carried above the height of the crossbar of the goal frame shall not be allowed.

  A goal scored by a defending player who strikes the puck with his stick carried above the height of the crossbar of the goal frame shall be allowed.

(d) Batting the puck above the normal height of the shoulders with a stick is prohibited. When a puck is struck with a high stick and subsequently comes into the possession of a teammate, there shall be a whistle. If a territorial advantage is gained by the offending Team, the ensuing face-off will be where the high-stick occurred. If a territorial disadvantage occurs to the offending Team, the ensuing face-off will be where the puck is touched. Play continues following a high-sticked puck if:

(1) the puck has been batted to an opponent in which case the play shall continue.

(2) a player of the defending side shall bat the puck into his own goal in which case the goal shall be allowed.

(NOTE) When a player bats the puck to an opponent under sub-section 1, the Referee shall give the "washout" signal immediately. Otherwise, he will stop the play.

(e) When either Team is below the numerical strength of its opponent and a player of the Team of greater numerical strength causes a stoppage of play by striking the puck with his stick above the height of his shoulder, the resulting face-off shall be made at one of the end zone face-off spots adjacent to the goal of the Team causing the stoppage.

Rule 62. Holding an Opponent

A minor penalty shall be imposed on a player who holds an opponent by using his hands, arms or legs.

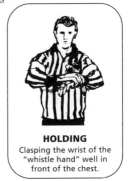

HOLDING
Clasping the wrist of the "whistle hand" well in front of the chest.

(NOTE) A player is permitted to use his arm in a strength move, by blocking his opponent, provided he has body position and is not using his hands in a holding manner, when doing so.

Rule 63. Holding an Opponent's Stick

A player is not permitted to hold an opponent's stick. A minor penalty shall be assessed to a player who holds an opponent's stick.

(NOTE) A player is permitted to protect himself by defending against an opponent's stick. He must immediately release the stick and allow the player to resume normal play.

Rule 64. Hooking

Hooking is the act of using the stick in a manner that enables a player to restrain an opponent.

(NOTE) When a player is checking another in such a way that there is only stick-to-stick contact, such action is not to be penalized as hooking.

HOOKING
A tugging motion with both arms, as if pulling something toward the stomach.

(a) A minor penalty shall be imposed on a player who impedes the progress of an opponent by "hooking" with his stick.

(b) A major penalty and a game misconduct shall be imposed on any player who injures an opponent by "hooking". A player who has been assessed a major penalty and a game misconduct under this Rule shall be automatically fined one hundred dollars ($100).

Rule 65. Icing the Puck

(a) For the purpose of this Rule, the center red line will divide the ice into halves. Should any player of a Team, equal or superior in numerical strength to the opposing Team, shoot, bat or deflect the puck from his own half of the ice beyond the goal line of the opposing Team, play shall be stopped and the puck faced-off at the end face-off spot of the offending Team, unless on the play, the puck shall have entered the net of the opposing Team, in which case the goal shall be allowed.

ICING
Linesman's arms folded across the upper chest.

For the purpose of this Rule, the point of last contact with the puck by the Team in possession shall be used to determine whether icing has occurred or not.

WASH-OUT
Both arms swung laterally at shoulder level with palms down. When used by the Linesman, it means no icing or no off-side.

(NOTE 1) If during the period of a delayed whistle due to a foul by a player of the side NOT in possession, the side in possession "ices" the puck, then the face-off following the stoppage of play shall take place in the neutral zone near the defending blue line of the Team icing the puck.

(NOTE 2) When a Team is "short-handed" as the result of a penalty and the penalty is about to expire, the decision as to whether there has been an "icing" shall be determined at the instant the penalty expires. The action of the penalized player remaining in the penalty box will not alter the ruling.

(NOTE 3) For the purpose of interpretation of the Rule, "icing the puck" is completed the instant the puck is touched first by a defending player (other than the goalkeeper) after it has crossed the goal line and if in the action of so touching the puck, it is knocked or deflected into the net, it is NO goal.

(NOTE 4) When the puck is shot and rebounds from the body or stick of an opponent in his own half of the ice so as to cross the goal line of the player shooting, it shall not be considered as "icing".

(NOTE 5) Notwithstanding the provisions of the section concerning "batting" the puck in respect to the "icing the puck" rule, the provisions of the final paragraph of Rule 59(e) apply and NO goal can be scored by batting the puck with the hand into the opponent's goal whether intended or not.

(NOTE 6) If while the Linesman has signalled a slow whistle for a clean interception under Rule 77(c), the player intercepting shoots or bats the puck beyond the opponent's goal line in such a manner as to constitute "icing the puck", the Linesman's "slow whistle" shall be considered exhausted the instant the puck crosses the blue line and "icing" shall be called in the usual manner.

(b) If a player of the side shooting the puck down the ice who is on-side and eligible to play the puck does so before it is touched by an opposing player, the play shall continue and it shall not be considered a violation of this Rule.

(c) If the puck was so shot by a player of a side below the numerical strength of the opposing Team, play shall continue and the icing violation shall not be called.

(NOTE) If the Team returns to full strength following a shot by one of its players, play shall continue and the face-off shall not take place.

(d) If, however, the puck shall go beyond the goal line in the opposite half of the ice directly from either of the players while facing-off, it shall not be considered a violation of this Rule.

(e) If, in the opinion of the Linesman, any player of the opposing Team is able to play the puck before it passes his goal line, but has not done so, play shall continue and the icing violation shall not be called. If, in the opinion of the Referee, the defending side intentionally abstains from playing the puck promptly when they are in a position to do so, he shall stop the play and order the resulting face-off on the adjacent corner face-off spot nearest the goal of the Team at fault. If, in the opinion of the Linesman, the goaltender leaves the crease on a potential icing and feigns playing the puck at any time, the potential icing shall not be called and play shall continue.

(NOTE) The purpose of this section is to enforce con-tinuous action and both Referee and Linesmen should interpret and apply the Rule to produce this result.

(f) If the puck touches any part of a player of the opposing side, including his skates or his stick, or if it passes through any part of the goal crease before it reaches the opposing Team's goal line, or if it touches any part of the opposing Team's goalkeeper, including his skates or his stick, at any time before or after crossing the goal line, it shall not be considered icing.

> *(NOTE) If a goalkeeper takes any action to dislodge the puck from the back of the net, icing shall be washed out.*

(g) If a goalkeeper has been removed from the playing surface for an extra player (Teams at equal or superior in numerical strength), the icing rule shall be in effect if the puck passes through or touches any part of the goal crease before it crosses the goal line.

(h) If the Linesman shall have erred in calling an "icing the puck" infraction (regardless of whether either Team is short-handed), the puck shall be faced-off on the center ice face-off spot.

Rule 66. Illegal Puck

If at any time while play is in progress, a puck other than the one legally in play shall appear on the playing surface, the play shall not be stopped but shall continue with the legal puck until the play then in progress is completed by change of possession.

Rule 67. Interference

This Rule shall be a point of emphasis for the 1999-2000 season.

(NOTE) A strict standard of interference must be adhered to in all areas of the rink, with emphasis on interference in the Neutral Zone.

INTERFERENCE
Crossed arms stationary in front of the chest with fists closed.

(a) A minor penalty shall be imposed on a player who interferes with or impedes the progress of an opponent who is not in possession of the puck.

(b) A minor penalty shall be imposed on a player who restrains an opponent who is attempting to "forecheck".

(c) A minor penalty shall be imposed on an attacking player who deliberately checks a defensive player, including the goalkeeper, who is not in possession of the puck.

(d) A minor penalty shall be imposed on a player who shall cause an opponent who is not in possession of the puck to be forced off-side, causing a stoppage in play.

(e) A minor penalty shall be imposed on a player who deliberately knocks a stick out of an opponent's hand, or who prevents a player who has dropped his stick or any other piece of equipment from regaining possession of it.

(f) A minor penalty shall be imposed on a player who knocks or shoots any abandoned or broken stick or illegal puck or other debris towards an opposing puck carrier in a manner that could cause him to be distracted. (See also Rule 88(a) – Throwing Stick.)

(g) A minor penalty shall be imposed on any player on the players' bench or penalty bench who, by means of his stick or his body, interferes with the movements of the puck or any opponent on the ice during the progress of the play.

(h) If, when the goalkeeper has been removed from the ice, any member of his Team (including the goalkeeper) not legally on the ice, including the Manager, Coach or Trainer, interferes by means of his body, stick or any other object with the movements of the puck or an opposing player, the Referee shall immediately award a goal to the non-offending Team.

(i) When a player in control of the puck on his opponent's side of the center red line and having no other opponent to pass than the goalkeeper is interfered with by a stick or any part thereof or any other object thrown or shot by any member of the defending Team including the Manager, Coach or Trainer, a penalty shot shall be awarded to the non-offending Team.

(NOTE 1)   Body Position:

Body position shall be determined as the player skating in front of or beside his opponent, traveling in the same direction. A player who is behind an opponent, who does not have the puck, may not use his stick or body in order to restrain his opponent, but must skate in order to gain or reestablish his proper position in order to make a check.

A player is allowed the ice he is standing on (body position) and is not required to move in order to let an opponent proceed. A player may "block" the path of an opponent provided he is doing so by skating in the same direction. Moving laterally and without establishing body position, then making contact with the non-puck carrier is not permitted and will be penalized as interference. A player is always entitled to use his body position to lengthen an opponent's path to the puck, provided his stick is not utilized; his free hand is not used and he does not take advantage of his body position to deliver an otherwise illegal check.

(NOTE 2)   Possession of the Puck:

The last player to touch the puck, other than the goalkeeper, shall be considered the player in possession. The player deemed in possession of the puck may be checked legally, provided the check is rendered immediately following his loss of possession.

(NOTE 3) Restrain:

The actions of a player who does not have body position, but instead uses illegal means (e.g. hook with stick; hold with hands) to impede an opponent who is not in possession of the puck. Illegal means are acts which allow a player to establish, maintain or restore body position, other than by skating.

(NOTE 4) Pick:

A "pick" is the action of a player who checks an opponent who is not in possession of the puck and is unaware of the impending check/hit. A player who is aware of an impending hit, not deemed to be a legal "battle for the puck", may not be interfered with by a player delivering a "pick". A player delivering a "pick" is one who moves into an opponent's path without initially having body position, thereby taking him out of the play.

(NOTE 5) Free Hand:

A free hand is the one that is not evident holding the player's own stick. Free hand use is permitted to "fend off" an opponent or his stick, but may not be used to hold an opponent's stick or body.

(NOTE 6) Stick:

Any reference made to the use of the stick implies any portion of the stick. It is generally accepted that the blade or end of the shaft are used in stick restraining tactics.

Rule 68. Interference by/with Spectators

(a) In the event of a player being held or interfered with by a spectator, the Referee or Linesman shall blow the whistle and play shall be stopped unless the Team of the player interfered with is in possession of the puck. The play shall be allowed to be completed before blowing the whistle and the puck shall be faced-off where play was stopped.

(b) Any player who physically interferes with the spectators shall automatically incur a gross misconduct penalty and the Referee shall report all such infractions to the Commissioner who shall have full power to impose such further penalty as he shall deem appropriate.

(c) In the event that objects are thrown on the ice that interfere with the progress of the game, the Referee shall blow the whistle and stop the play and the puck shall be faced-off at the spot where play is stopped.

> *(NOTE 1) In the event that objects are thrown on the ice during a stoppage in play, including after the scoring of a goal, a bench minor penalty will be assessed to the home Team.*

> *(NOTE 2) The Referee shall report to the Commissioner for disciplinary action all cases in which a player becomes involved in an altercation with a spectator.*

Rule 69. Kicking a Player

A match penalty shall be imposed on any player who kicks or attempts to kick another player.

Whether or not an injury occurs, the Referee will impose a five (5) minute time penalty under this Rule. Refer to Rule 43 – Attempt to Injure or Rule 52 – Deliberate Injury of an Opponent.

Rule 70. Kicking the Puck

(a) Kicking the puck shall be permitted in all zones. A goal cannot be scored by an attacking player who uses a distinct kicking motion to propel the puck into the net. A goal cannot be scored by an attacking player who kicks a puck that deflects into the net off any player, goalkeeper or Official.

(b) A puck that deflects into the net off of an attacking player who does not use a distinct kicking motion, is a legitimate goal.

(c) A goal cannot be scored by an attacking player who kicks any equipment (stick, glove, helmet, etc.) at the puck, causing the puck to cross the goal line.

Rule 71. Kneeing

Kneeing is the act of a player making a distinct movement of his knee.

A minor, major or match penalty shall be imposed on any player who fouls an opponent by kneeing

When a player has been assessed a

KNEEING
Slapping the knee with palm of hand while keeping both skates on the ice.

major penalty for kneeing he shall also be
assessed a Game Misconduct.

Rule 72. Leaving the Players' or Penalty Bench

(a) No player may leave the players' or penalty
bench at any time during an altercation or for
the purpose of starting an altercation.
Substitutions made prior to the altercation
shall be permitted provided the players so
substituting do not enter the altercation. A
player who has entered the game on a legal
line change and starts an altercation will be
subjected to discipline in accordance with
Rule 33A – Supplementary Discipline.

(b) For violation of this Rule, a game misconduct
penalty shall be imposed on the player who was
the first or second player to leave the players'
or penalty bench from either or both Teams.

(c) The first player to leave the players' or penalty
bench from either or both Teams shall be
suspended automatically without pay for the
next ten (10) regular League and/or playoff
games of his Team.

(d) The second player to leave the bench from
either or both Teams shall be suspended
automatically without pay for the next five (5)
regular League and/or playoff games.

> *(NOTE) The determination as to the players penal-
> ized under (c) and (d) of this Rule shall be made
> by the Referee in consultation with the Linesmen
> and Off-Ice officials. In the event that he is unable to
> identify the offending players, the matter will be
> referred to the Commissioner or his designee and
> such determinations may be made subsequently*

> *based on reports and other information including*
> *but not limited to television tapes.*

(e) Any Team that has a player penalized under
(a) shall be fined ten thousand dollars
($10,000) for the first instance. This fine shall
be increased by five thousand dollars ($5,000)
for each subsequent occurrence over the next
following three-year period.

(f) All players including the first and second
players who leave the bench during an
altercation shall be subject to an automatic
fine in the amount equal to the maximum
permitted under the collective bargaining
agreement.

(g) Any player who leaves the penalty bench
during an altercation and is not the first player
to do so, shall be suspended automatically
without pay for the next five (5) regular
League and/or playoff games.

(h) Except at the end of each period or on
expiration of his penalty, no player may, at any
time, leave the penalty bench.

(i) A penalized player who leaves the penalty
bench before his penalty has expired, whether
play is in progress or not, shall incur an
additional minor penalty, after serving his
unexpired penalty.

(j) Any penalized player leaving the penalty bench
during stoppage of play and during an
altercation shall incur a minor penalty plus a
game misconduct penalty after serving his
unexpired time.

(k) If a player leaves the penalty bench before his

penalty is fully served, the Penalty Timekeeper shall note the time and signal the Officials who will stop play when the offending player's Team obtains possession of the puck.

(l) In the case of a player returning to the ice before his time has expired through an error of the Penalty Timekeeper, he is not to serve an additional penalty, but must serve his unexpired time.

(m) If a player of the attacking side in possession of the puck shall be in such a position as to have no opposition between him and the opposing goalkeeper, and while in such position he shall be interfered with by a player of the opposing side who shall have illegally entered the game, the Referee shall impose a penalty shot against the side to which the offending player belongs.

(n) If the opposing goalkeeper has been removed and a player throws or shoots any part of a stick or any other object at the puck or puck carrier, or if the puck carrier is fouled from behind, thereby being prevented from having a clear shot on an open goal, a goal shall be awarded to the attacking Team.

If, when the opposing goalkeeper has been removed from the ice, a player of the side attacking the unattended goal is interfered with by a player who shall have entered the game illegally, the Referee shall immediately award a goal to the non-offending Team.

(o) If a Coach or Manager gets on the ice after the start of a period and before that period is

---

ended, the Referee shall impose a bench minor penalty against the Team and report the incident to the Commissioner for disciplinary action.

(p) Any club executive or Manager committing the same offense will be automatically fined two hundred dollars ($200).

(q) If a penalized player returns to the ice from the penalty bench before his penalty has expired by his own error or the error of the Penalty Timekeeper, any goal scored by his own Team while he is illegally on the ice shall be disallowed but all penalties imposed on either Team shall be served as regular penalties.

(r) If a player shall illegally enter the game from his own players' bench or from the penalty bench, any goal scored by his own Team while he is illegally on the ice shall be disallowed but all penalties imposed on either Team shall be served as regular penalties.

(s) A bench minor penalty shall be imposed on a Team whose player(s) leave the players' bench for any purpose other than a change of players and when no altercation is in progress.

(t) Any player who has been ordered to the dressing room by the Officials and returns to his bench or to the ice surface for any reason before the appropriate time shall be assessed a game misconduct and shall be suspended automatically without pay for the next ten (10) regular League and/or playoff games.

(u) The Coach(es) of the Team(s) whose player(s) left the players' bench(es) during an altercation may be suspended, pending a review by the Commissioner. The Coach(es) also may be fined a maximum of ten thousand dollars ($10,000).

(v) For all suspensions imposed on players under this Rule, the club of the player shall pay to the League a sum equal to the pro-rata of that player's salary covered by the suspension. For purposes of computing amounts due for a player's suspension, the player's fixed salary shall be divided by the number of days in the regular season and then, said result shall be multiplied by the number of games suspended.

In addition, any club that is deemed by the Commissioner to pay or reimburse to the player the amount of the fine or loss of salary assessed under this Rule shall be fined automatically one hundred thousand dollars ($100,000).

(NOTE) In the event that suspensions imposed under this Rule cannot be completed in regular League and/or playoff games in any one season, the remainder of the suspension shall be served the following season.

Rule 73. Obscene or Profane Language or Gestures

(a) Players shall not use obscene gestures on the ice or anywhere in the rink before, during or after the game. For violation of this Rule, a game misconduct penalty shall be imposed and the Referee shall report the circumstances to

the Commissioner of the League for further
disciplinary action.

(b) Players shall not use profane language on the
ice or anywhere in the rink before, during or
after a game. For violation of this Rule, a
misconduct penalty shall be imposed except
when the violation occurs in the vicinity of the
players' bench in which case a bench minor
penalty shall be imposed.

> *(NOTE) It is the responsibility of all game officials*
> *and all club officials to send a confidential report*
> *to the Commissioner setting out the full details*
> *concerning the use of obscene gestures or language*
> *by any player, Coach or other official. The*
> *Commissioner shall take such further disciplinary*
> *action as he shall deem appropriate.*

(c) Club Executives, Managers, Coaches and
Trainers shall not use obscene or profane
language or gestures anywhere in the rink. For
violation of this Rule, a bench minor penalty
shall be imposed.

Rule 74. Off-Sides

(a) The position of the player's skates and not that
of his stick shall be the determining factor in
all instances in deciding an off-side. A player is
off-side when both skates are completely over
the outer edge of the determining center line
or blue line involved in the play.

> *(NOTE 1) A player is on-side when either of his*
> *skates are in contact with, or on his own side of the*
> *line, at the instant the puck completely crosses the*
> *outer edge of that line regardless of the position of*
> *his stick.*

(NOTE 2) It should be noted that while the position of the player's skates is what determines whether a player is "off-side", nevertheless the question of an "off-side" never arises until the puck has completely crossed the outer edge of the line at which time the decision is to be made.

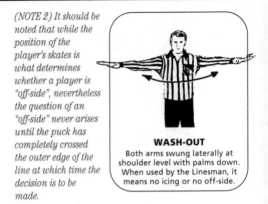

WASH-OUT
Both arms swung laterally at shoulder level with palms down. When used by the Linesman, it means no icing or no off-side.

(b) If in the opinion of the Linesman, an intentional off-side play has been made, the puck shall be faced-off at the end face-off spot in the defending zone of the offending Team.

> *(NOTE 1) An intentional off-side is one which is made for the purpose of securing a stoppage of play regardless of the reason, whether either Team is short-handed.*

> *(NOTE 2) If, while an off-side call is delayed, a player of the offending Team deliberately touches the puck to create a stoppage of play, the Linesman will signal an intentional off-side.*

(c) If a Linesman errs in calling an off-side pass infraction (regardless of whether either Team is short-handed), the puck shall be faced-off on the center ice face-off spot.

Rule 75. Passes

(a) The puck may be passed by any player to a player on the same Team within any one of the three zones into which the ice is divided. It may not be passed

---

forward from a player in one zone to a player on the same Team in another zone, except by players of the defending Team who may make and take forward passes from their own defending zone to the center line without incurring an off-side penalty. This forward pass from the defending zone must be completed by the pass receiver who is preceded by the puck across the center line, otherwise the play shall be stopped and the face-off shall be at the point from which the pass was made.

> *(NOTE 1) The position of the puck and not that of the player's skates shall be the determining factor in deciding from which zone the pass was made.*

> *(NOTE 2) Passes may be completed legally at the center red line in exactly the same manner as passes at the attacking blue line.*

> *(NOTE 3) In the event the player has preceded the puck at the center line he may become eligible to play the puck if he makes skate contact with the line prior to playing the puck.*

(b) Should the puck, after having been passed, contact any part of the body, stick or skate of a player on the Team who is legally on-side, the pass shall be considered complete.

(c) The player last touched by the puck shall be deemed to be in possession.

Rebounds off goalkeepers' pads or other equipment shall not be considered as a change of possession or completion of the play by the Team when applying Rule 33(b) – Calling of Penalties.

(d) If a player in the neutral zone is preceded in the attacking zone by the puck passed from the neutral zone, he shall be eligible to take possession of the puck anywhere in the attacking zone except when the "icing the puck" Rule applies.

(e) If a player in the same zone from which a pass is made is preceded by the puck into succeeding zones, he shall be eligible to take possession of the puck in that zone except where the "icing the puck" Rule applies.

(f) If an attacking player passes the puck backward toward his own goal from the attacking zone, an opponent may play the puck anywhere regardless of whether the opponent was in the same zone at the time the puck was passed. (No "slow whistle".)

Rule 76. Physical Abuse of Officials

(a) Any player who deliberately applies physical force in any manner against an Official, in any manner attempts to injure an Official, physically demeans, or deliberately applies physical force to an Official solely for the purpose of getting free of such an Official during or immediately following an altercation shall receive a game misconduct penalty.

In addition, the following disciplinary penalties shall apply:

CATEGORY I

Any player who deliberately strikes an Official and causes injury or who deliberately applies physical force in any manner against an Official with intent to injure, or who in any manner attempts to injure an Official shall be automatically suspended for not less than 20 games. (For the purpose of the Rule, "intent to injure" shall mean any physical force which a player knew or should have known could reasonably be expected to cause injury.)

CATEGORY II

Any player who deliberately applies physical force to an Official in any manner (excluding actions as set out in Category One), which physical force is applied without intent to injure, shall be automatically suspended for not less than ten (10) games.

CATEGORY III

Any player who, by his actions, physically demeans an Official or who deliberately applies physical force to an Official solely for the purpose of getting free of such an Official during or immediately following an altercation shall be suspended for not less than three (3) games.

Immediately after the game in which such game misconduct penalty is imposed, the

Referee shall, in consultation with the Linesmen, decide the category of the offense. He shall make an oral report to the Commissioner and advise of the category and of the offense. In addition, he shall file a written report to the Commissioner in which he may request a review as to the adequacy of the suspension. The player and club involved shall be notified of the decision of the Referee on the morning following the game and the player may request the Commissioner to review, subject to the provisions of this Rule, the penalty imposed by the Referee. Such request must be filed with the Commissioner in writing not later than seventy-two (72) hours following notification of the penalty. No appeal to the Board of Governors pursuant to By-Law 17 shall be available to the player unless a review has been conducted as provided herein.

If a review of the incident is requested by either the player or by the Official, a hearing will be conducted by the Commissioner as soon as practical prior to the fourth game of any suspension. The player's suspension shall continue pending the outcome of the hearing by the Commissioner.

After any review as called for hereby, the Commissioner shall issue an order either:

(1) sustaining the minimum suspension, or . . .

(2) increasing the number of games within the

category, or . . .

(3) changing to a lower category, or . . .

(4) changing to a lower category and increasing the number of games within the category.

A player shall have the right of appeal from any such order pursuant to By-Law 17.11. Upon such appeal, the Board of Governors' determination shall be one of the four alternatives listed above.

The penalties imposed under this Rule shall not be deemed to limit the right of the Commissioner with respect to any action that he might otherwise take under By-Law 17.

In the event that the player has committed more than one offense under this Rule, in addition to the penalties imposed under this offense, his case shall be referred to the Commissioner of the League for consideration of supplementary disciplinary action.

(In all instances where the Commissioner is referred to in this Rule, it shall mean the Commissioner or his designee.)

(b) Any Club Executive, Manager, Coach or Trainer who holds or strikes an Official shall be automatically suspended from the game, ordered to the dressing room and the matter will be reported to the Commissioner for further disciplinary action.

Rule 77. Preceding Puck into Attacking Zone

All players must be clear of the attacking zone (skate contact with the blue line) prior to a puck being shot into that zone. The opportunity to "tag" and return into the zone has been removed, and only when the defensive Team brings the puck into the neutral zone, can they be legally checked without an off-side or stoppage being called for failing to advance the puck.

(a) Players of the attacking Team must not precede the puck into the attacking zone.

(b) For violation of this Rule, the play is stopped and the puck shall be faced-off in the neutral zone at the face-off spot nearest the attacking zone of the offending Team.

> *(NOTE) A player actually controlling the puck who shall cross the line ahead of the puck shall not be considered "off-side".*

(c) For all delayed off-sides, including intentional off-sides, the Linesman will raise his non-whistle arm. He will allow play to continue and, if a stoppage of play occurs, there will be three possible face-off locations:

(1) When an intentional off-

SLOW WHISTLE

Arm in which the whistle is not held extended above head. If play returns to neutral zone without stoppage of play, arm is drawn down the instant the puck crosses the line.

side has been called, the face-off location will be on the face-off spot of the offending team's defensive zone.

(2) If an errant pass is not intercepted by the defending player, the whistle shall be blown and the ensuing face-off shall take place at the location from where the pass or shot originated.

(3) If the puck is intercepted by the defending player and he is checked, losing puck control, the ensuing face-off shall take place on a neutral zone face-off spot nearest to the defending Team's blue line.

(NOTES:)

(i) An intentional off-side is one which is made for the purpose of securing a stoppage of play regardless of the reason.

(ii) If, while an off-side call is delayed, a player of the offending Team deliberately touches the puck to create a stoppage of play, the Linesman will signal an intentional off-side.

(iii) An intentional off-side is still in effect when a team is short-handed. A defensive player, who is in position to play the puck into the zone, should play the puck or the ensuing face-off will be conducted where the shot originated.

(iv) If icing is signaled and off-side occurs on the same play, the off-side will be called.

(v) If a delayed off-side has been signaled, the non-offending player must carry or pass the puck towards and into the neutral zone. If he does not, the whistle shall be blown and the face-off take place in the neutral zone at

---

> *a spot nearest the defending Team's blue line.*
>
> *(vi) If, in the judgement of the Linesman, the attacking player(s) are making an effort to exit the attacking zone and are in close proximity to the blue line at the time the puck is shot into the zone, the play will not be deemed to be an intentional off-side.*
>
> *(vii)If the puck is shot at the goal and is not intercepted, this may be deemed to be an intentional off-side.*
>
> *(viii)A puck that deflects back into the defensive zone off of an Official who is in the neutral zone will be off-side.*

  (d) If a player legally carries or passes the puck back into his own defensive zone while a player of the opposing Team is in such defensive zone, the off-side shall be ignored and play permitted to continue. (No slow whistle.)

> *(NOTE) If a puck clearly deflects off a defensive player in the neutral zone back into the defensive zone, all attacking players are eligible to play the puck.*

Rule 78. Protection of Goalkeeper

The revised crease rule is intended to implement a "no harm, no foul, no video review" standard. The rule is based on the premise that an attacking player's position, whether inside or outside the crease, should not, by itself, determine whether a goal should be allowed or disallowed - i.e., goals scored while attacking players are standing in the crease may, in appropriate circumstances be allowed. Goals should be disallowed only if:

(1) an attacking player, either by his positioning or by contact, impairs the goalkeeper's ability to move freely within his crease or defend his goal; or (2) an attacking player initiates more than incidental contact with a goalkeeper, inside or outside of his goal crease. Incidental contact with a goalkeeper will be permitted, and resulting goals allowed, when such contact is initiated outside of the goal crease, provided the attacking player has made a reasonable effort to avoid such contact. The rule will be enforced exclusively in accordance with the on-ice judgement of the Referee(s), and not by means of video replay or review.

NEW

(a) If an attacking player initiates contact with a goalkeeper, incidental or otherwise, while the goalkeeper is in his goal crease, and a goal is scored, the goal will be disallowed.

NEW

(b) If an attacking player initiates any contact with a goalkeeper, other than incidental contact, while the goalkeeper is outside his goal crease, and a goal is scored, the goal will be disallowed.

NEW

(c) In all cases in which an attacking player initiates other than incidental contact with a goalkeeper, whether or not the goalkeeper is inside or outside the goal crease, and whether or not a goal is scored, the offensive player will receive a penalty (minor or major, as the Referee deems appropriate). See also rule 51(c) – Charging).

(NOTE 1) In exercising his judgment under subsections (a) and (b) above, the Referee should give more significant consideration to the degree and nature of the contact with the goalkeeper than to the exact location of the goalkeeper at the time of the contact.

(NOTE 2) If an attacking player has been pushed, shoved, or fouled by a defending player so as to cause him to come into contact with the goalkeeper, such contact will not be deemed to be contact initiated by the attacking player for purposes of this rule, provided the attacking player has made a reasonable effort to avoid such contact.

(NOTE 3) A goalkeeper is not "fair game" just because he is outside the goal crease. The appropriate penalty should be assessed in every case where an attacking player makes unnecessary contact with the goalkeeper. However, incidental contact will be permitted when the goalkeeper is in the act of playing the puck outside his goal crease provided the attacking player has made a reasonable effort to avoid such unnecessary contact.

NEW (d) If (i) a goalkeeper initiates contact with an offensive player who is in the goal crease; and (ii) such contact is (a) initiated by the goalkeeper in order to establish position in his goal crease; and (b) results in an impairment of the goalkeeper's ability to defend his goal, and a goal is scored, the goal will be disallowed.

NEW (e) If, after any contact by a goalkeeper who is attempting to establish position in his goal crease, the attacking player does not immediately vacate his current position in the goal crease (i.e. give ground to the goalkeeper), and a goal is scored, the goal will be disallowed. In all such cases, whether or not a goal is scored, the offensive player will receive a minor penalty for goalkeeper interference.

(NOTE 4) The overriding rationale of subsections (d) and (e) above is that a goalkeeper should have the ability to move freely within his goal crease without being hindered by the actions of an attacking player.

(NOTE 5) If, while attempting to establish position within his goal crease, a goalkeeper commits an act that is worthy of a penalty (i.e. cross-checking, slashing, etc.), then the appropriate penalty shall be assessed by the Referee.

NEW

(f) When a goalkeeper has played the puck outside of his crease and is then prevented from returning to his crease area due to the deliberate actions of an attacking player, such player may be penalized for goalkeeper interference. Similarly, the goalkeeper may be penalized, if by his actions outside of his crease he deliberately interferes with an attacking player who is attempting to play the puck or an opponent.

NEW

(g) If an attacking player establishes a significant position within the goal crease, so as to obstruct the goalkeeper's vision and impair his ability to defend his goal, and a goal is scored, the goal will be disallowed.

(NOTE 6) For this purpose, a player "establishes a significant position within the crease" when, in the Referee's judgment, his body, or a substantial portion thereof, is within the goal crease for more than an instantaneous period of time.

NEW

(h) Subject to (i) below, if an attacking player enters the goal crease and, by his actions, impairs the goalkeeper's ability to defend his goal, and a goal is scored, the goal will be disallowed.

NEW

(i) In a rebound situation, or where a goalkeeper and offensive player(s) are simultaneously attempting to play a loose puck, whether inside or outside the crease, incidental contact with the goalkeeper will be permitted, and any goal that is scored as a result thereof will be allowed.

NEW

(j) In the event that a goalkeeper has been pushed into the net together with the puck after making a stop, the goal will be disallowed. If applicable, appropriate penalties will be assessed.

NEW

(k) A goalkeeper who deliberately initiates contact with an attacking player other than to establish position in the crease, or who otherwise acts to create the appearance of other than incidental contact with an attacking player, is subject to the assessment of a minor penalty for unsportsmanlike conduct.

NEW

(l) An attacking player who, in the judgment of the Referee, initiates contact with the goalkeeper, whether inside or outside the crease, in a fashion that would otherwise warrant a penalty, will be assessed an appropriate penalty (minor or major and/or game misconduct) and will be subject to additional sanctions as appropriate pursuant to Rule 33A – Supplementary Discipline.

(NOTE 7) For purposes of this rule, "contact", whether incidental or otherwise, shall mean any contact that is made between or among a goalkeeper and attacking player(s), whether by means of a stick or any part of the body.

(NOTE 8) The above-stated standards relating to when a goal will be disallowed will be applied in all situations in which the puck enters the net regardless of whether it was directed into the net by the attacking or defensive team.

Rule 79. Puck Must Be Kept in Motion

(a) The puck must be kept in motion at all times.

(b) A minor penalty shall be imposed on any player, including the goalkeeper, who holds, freezes or plays the puck with his stick, skates or body in such a manner as to deliberately cause a stoppage of play.

> *(NOTE) With regard to a goalkeeper, this Rule applies outside of his goal crease area.*

Rule 80. Puck Out of Bounds or Unplayable

(a) When a puck goes outside the playing area at either end or either side of the rink, or strikes any obstacles above the playing surface other than the boards or glass, it shall be faced-off where it was shot or deflected out of play.

Notwithstanding this Rule, should an attacking player cause the puck to go out of play or become unplayable in the attacking zone, the face-off shall take place at a neutral zone face-off spot or the point from which the puck left the ice, whichever is less advantageous to the attacking Team.

Any loss of time on the game or penalty clocks due to the puck going out of play must be replaced. The Video Goal Judge may be consulted to ensure the time is replaced accurately.

(b) When the puck becomes lodged in the netting on the outside of either goal so as to make it unplayable, or if it is "frozen" between opposing players intentionally or otherwise, the Referee shall stop the play and face-off the puck at either of the adjacent face-off spots unless in the opinion of the Referee, the stoppage was caused by the attacking Team, in which case the resulting face-off shall be conducted in the neutral zone.

> *(NOTE) The defending Team and/or the attacking Team may play the puck off the net at any time. However, should the puck remain on the net for more than three (3) seconds, play shall be stopped and the face-off shall take place in the end zone, corner face-off spot, except when the stoppage is caused by the attacking Team, in which case the face-off shall take place on a face-off spot in the neutral zone.*

(c) A minor penalty shall be imposed on a goalkeeper who deliberately drops the puck on the goal netting to cause a stoppage of play.

(d) If the puck comes to rest on top of the boards surrounding the playing area, it shall be considered to be in play and may be played legally by hand or stick.

Rule 81. Puck Out of Sight

Should a scramble take place or a player accidentally fall on the puck and the puck be out of sight of the Referee, he shall immediately blow his whistle and stop the play. The puck shall then be faced-off at the point where the play was stopped unless otherwise provided for in the Rules.

Rule 82. Puck Striking Official

(a) Play shall not be stopped if the puck touches an Official anywhere on the rink, regardless of whether a Team is shorthanded or not. A puck that deflects back into the defensive zone off an Official who is in the neutral zone, will be deemed to be off-side as per Rule 74 – Off-Sides.

(b) When a puck deflects off an Official and goes out of play, the ensuing face-off will take place at the spot where the puck deflected off the Official.

> *(NOTE) If a goal is scored as a result of being deflected directly into the net off an Official, the goal shall not be allowed.*

Rule 83. Refusing to Start Play

(a) If, when both Teams are on the ice, one Team for any reason shall refuse to play when ordered to do so by the Referee, he shall warn the Captain and allow the Team so refusing fifteen (15) seconds within which to begin the play or resume play. If at the end of that time, the Team shall still refuse to play, the Referee shall impose a two-minute penalty on a player of the offending Team to be designated by the Manager or Coach of that Team through the playing Captain. Should there be a repetition of the same incident, the Referee shall notify the Manager or Coach that he has been fined the sum of two hundred dollars ($200). Should the offending Team still refuse to play, the Referee shall have no alternative but to declare that the game be forfeited to the non-offending club and the case shall be reported to the Commissioner for further action.

(b) If a Team, when ordered to do so by the Referee through its club executive, Manager or Coach, fails to go on the ice and start play within five (5) minutes, the club executive, Manager or Coach shall be fined five hundred dollars ($500), the game shall be forfeited and the case shall be reported to the Commissioner for further action.

> *(NOTE) The Commissioner of the League shall issue instructions pertaining to records, etc., of a forfeited game.*

Rule 84. Roughing

Roughing is a minor altercation that is not worthy of a major penalty to either participant. (An altercation is a situation involving two players, with at least one to be penalized.

ROUGHING
A thrusting motion with the arm extending from the side.

A minor penalty shall be imposed on a player who strikes an opponent. (See also Rule 56 – Fisticuffs.)

Rule 85. Slashing

Slashing is the act of swinging a player's stick at an opponent, whether contact is made or not.

(NOTE) Non aggressive stick contact to the pant or front of the shin pads, should not be penalized as slashing.

SLASHING
A chopping motion with the edge of one hand across the opposite forearm.

(a) A minor or major and a game misconduct penalty, at the discretion of the Referee, shall be imposed on any player who impedes the progress of an opponent by "slashing" with his stick.

(b) A major and a game misconduct penalty shall be imposed on any player who injures an opponent by slashing.

(c) Any player who swings his stick at another player in the course of an altercation shall be subject to a fine of not less than two hundred dollars ($200), with or without suspension, to be imposed by the Commissioner. (See Rule 43 – Attempt to Injure or Rule 52 – Deliberate Injury of Opponents.)

Rule 86. Spearing

Spearing shall mean stabbing an opponent with the point of the stick blade whether contact is made or not.

SPEARING
A jabbing motion with both hands thrust out in front of the body.

(a) A double minor penalty will be imposed on a player who spears an opponent and does not make contact.

(b) A major and a game misconduct shall be imposed on a player who spears an opponent. (See also Rule 43 – Attempt to Injure.)

(c) A match penalty shall be imposed on a player who injures an opponent as a result of a spear. (See also Rule 52 – Deliberate Injury of Opponents.)

Rule 87. Start of Game and Periods

(a) The game shall be commenced at the time scheduled by a "face-off" in the center of the rink and shall be renewed promptly at the conclusion of each intermission in the same manner.

No delay shall be permitted by reason of any ceremony, exhibition, demonstration or presentation unless consented to reasonably in advance by the visiting Team.

(b) Home clubs shall have the choice of goals to defend at the start of the game except where both players' benches are on the same side of the rink, in which case the home club shall start the game defending the goal nearest to its own bench. The Teams shall change ends for each period of regulation time and, in the playoffs, for each period of overtime. (See Rule 89 – NOTE – Tied Games)

(c) During the pre-game warm-up (which shall not exceed twenty (20) minutes in duration) and before the commencement of play in any period, each Team shall confine its activity to its own end of the rink. Refer to Rule 56(g) – Fisticuffs.

> *(NOTE 1) The Game Timekeeper shall be responsible for signalling the commencement and termination of the pre-game warm-up and any violation of this Rule by the players shall be reported to the Commissioner by the Supervisor when in attendance at the game.*

> *(NOTE 2) Players shall not be permitted to come on the ice during a stoppage of play or at the end of the first and second periods for the purpose of warming-up. The Referee will report any violation of this Rule to the Commissioner for disciplinary action.*

(d) Twenty (20) minutes before the time scheduled for the start of the game, both Teams shall vacate the ice and proceed to their dressing rooms while the ice is being flooded. Both Teams shall be signalled by the Game Timekeeper to return to the ice together in time for the scheduled start of the game.

(e) At the beginning of the game, if a Team fails to

appear on the ice promptly without proper justification, a fine shall be assessed against the offending Team, the amount of the fine to be decided by the Commissioner.

At the beginning of the second and third periods, and overtime periods in playoffs (0:00 on the clock), clubs must be on the ice or be observed to be proceeding to the ice. Failure to comply with this regulation will result in a two (2) minute bench minor penalty for delay of game.

(f) At the end of each period, the home Team players must proceed directly to their dressing room while the visiting Team players must wait for a signal from the Referee to proceed only if they have to go on the ice to reach their dressing room. Failure to comply with this regulation will result in a two (2) minute bench minor for delay of game.

Rule 88. Throwing Stick

(a) When any member of the defending Team, including any Manager, Coach or Trainer, deliberately throws or shoots any part of a stick or any other object at the puck or puck carrier in his defending zone, the Referee shall allow the play to be completed and if a goal is not scored, a penalty shot shall be awarded to the non-offending Team. This shot shall be taken by the player designated by the Referee as the player fouled.

If, when the opposing goalkeeper has been

removed, a member of the defending Team, including any Manager, Coach or Trainer, deliberately throws or shoots any part of a stick or any other object at the puck or puck carrier, thereby preventing the puck carrier from having a clear shot on an "open net", a goal shall be awarded to the attacking side.

> *(NOTE 1) If the Officials are unable to determine the person against whom the offense was made, the offended Team, through the Captain, shall designate a player on the ice at the time the offense was committed to take the shot.*
>
> *(NOTE 2) For the purpose of this Rule, an "open net" is defined as one from which a goalkeeper has been removed for an additional attacking player.*

(b) A minor penalty shall be imposed on any player on the ice who throws his stick or any part thereof or any other object in the direction of the puck in any zone, except when such act has been penalized by the assessment of a penalty shot or the award of a goal.

> *(NOTE) When the player discards the broken portion of a stick by tossing it to the side of the ice (and not over the boards) in such a way as will not interfere with play or opposing player, no penalty will be imposed for so doing.*

(c) A misconduct or game misconduct penalty, at the discretion of the Referee, shall be imposed on a player who throws his stick or any part thereof outside the playing area. If the offense is committed in protest of an Official's decision, a minor penalty for unsportsmanlike conduct plus a game misconduct penalty shall be assessed to the offending player.

Rule 89. Tied Game

(a) During League games, if at the end of the three (3) regular twenty (20) minute periods, the score shall be tied, each team shall be awarded one point in the League standings.

The teams will then play an additional overtime period of not more than five (5) minutes with the team scoring first declared the winner and being awarded an additional point. The overtime period shall be played with each team at a numerical strength of four (4) skaters and one (1) goalkeeper. Additional penalties to be assessed consistent with the rules in regulation time.

(NOTE 1) If a team is penalized in overtime, teams play 4-3.

(NOTE 2) In overtime, if a team is penalized such that a two-man advantage is called for, then the offending team will remain at three (3) skaters while the non-offending team will be permitted a fifth skater.

(NOTE 3) At the first stoppage of play after the two-man advantage is no longer in effect, the numerical strength of the team will revert back to either a 4 on 4 or a 4 on 3 situation, as appropriate.

(NOTE 4) If there is a man power advantage situation which carries over from regulation time to overtime, the above criteria will be applied at the start of overtime. Accordingly, if at the end of

*regulation time, the teams are 5 on 4,
overtime begins at 4 on 3.*

*(NOTE 5) A team shall be allowed to pull its
goalkeeper in favor of an additional skater
in the overtime period. However, should
that team lose the game during the time in
which the goalkeeper has been removed, it
would forfeit the automatic point gained in
the tie at the end of regulation play, except if
the goalkeeper has been removed at the call
of a delayed penalty against the other team.*

*(NOTE 6) The overtime period will be
commenced immediately following a two
(2) minute rest period during which the
players will remain on the ice. The Teams
will not change ends for the overtime period.*

*(NOTE 7) When the regulation ends with an on-
ice manpower strength of 5 on 3, teams will
commence the overtime with a strength of 5
on 3. With the expiration of penalties, due
to continuous action, player strength may
get to 5 on 5 or 5 on 4. At the first stoppage
of play following, player strength must be
adjusted to 4 on 4 or 4 on 3.*

*(NOTE 8) If at the end of regulation time teams
are 3 on 3, overtime starts 3 on 3. Once
player strength reaches 5 on 4 or 5 on 5, at
the next stoppage player strength is
adjusted to 4 on 3 or 4 on 4, as appropriate.*

*(NOTE 9) If at the end of regulation time teams
are 4 on 4 with a player or players in the
box serving non-coincidental penalties,
overtime starts 4 on 4 and players exit
penalty box as normal to 5 on 4 or 5 on 5.
At first stoppage of play, teams are adjusted
to 4 on 3 or 4 on 4, as appropriate.*

(b) Special conditions for the duration and number of periods of playoff games shall be arranged by the Board of Governors.

Rule 90. Time of Match

(a) The time allowed for a game shall be three (3) twenty-minute periods of actual play with a rest intermission between periods.

Play shall be resumed promptly following each intermission upon the expiration of fifteen (15) minutes or a length of time designated by the League from the completion of play in the preceding period. Timing of the intermission commences immediately upon the players and Officials leaving the playing surface. (See Rule 40(b) – Game Timekeeper.) A preliminary warning shall be given by the Game Timekeeper to the Officials and to both Teams five minutes prior to the resumption of play in each period and the final warning shall be given two minutes prior to resumption of play to enable the Teams to start play promptly.

(NOTE) For the purpose of keeping the spectators informed as to the time remaining during intermissions, the Game Timekeeper will use the electric clock to record length of intermissions.

(b) The Team scoring the greatest number of goals during the three (3) twenty-minute periods shall be the winner and shall be credited with two points in the League standings.

(c) In the interval between periods, the ice surface shall be flooded unless mutually agreed to the

---

contrary.

(d) If any unusual delay occurs within five (5) minutes of the end of the first or second periods, the Referee may order the next regular intermission to be taken immediately. The balance of the period will be completed on the resumption of play with the Teams defending the same goals after which, the Teams will change ends and resume play of the ensuing period without delay.

> *(NOTE) If a delay takes place with more than five (5) minutes remaining in the first or second period, the Referee will order the next regular intermission to be taken immediately only when requested to do so by the home club.*

Rule 91. Tripping

(NOTE 1) Accidental trips which occur simultaneously with a completed play will not be penalized.

(NOTE 2) If, in the opinion of the Referee, a player is unquestionably hook-checking the puck and obtains possession of it, thereby tripping the puck carrier, no penalty shall be imposed.

TRIPPING
Strike the right leg with the right hand below the knee keeping both skates on the ice.

(NOTE 3) Accidental trips occurring simultaneously with or after a stoppage of play will not be penalized.

(a) A minor penalty shall be imposed on any player who shall place his stick or any portion of his body in such a manner that it shall cause his opponent to trip and fall.

(b) When a player, in control of the puck on the opponent's side of the center red line and having no other opponent to pass than the goalkeeper, is tripped or otherwise fouled from behind, thus preventing a reasonable scoring opportunity, a penalty shot shall be awarded to the non-offending side. Nevertheless, the Referee shall not stop play until the attacking side has lost possession of the puck to the defending side.

> *(NOTE 4) The intention of this Rule is to restore a reasonable scoring opportunity which has been lost by reason of a foul from behind when the foul is committed on the opponent's side of the red line.*
>
> *"Control of the puck" means the act of propelling the puck with the stick. If while it is being propelled, the puck is touched by another player or his equipment, or hits the goal or goes free, the player shall no longer be considered to be "in control of the puck".*

(c) If, when the opposing goaltender has been removed from the ice, a player in control of the puck is tripped or otherwise fouled with no opposition between him and the opposing goal, thus preventing a reasonable scoring opportunity, the Referee shall immediately stop play and award a goal to the attacking Team.

Rule 92. Time-Outs

Each Team shall be permitted to take one thirty-second time-out during the course of any game, regular-season or playoffs. This time-out must be taken during a normal stoppage of play. Any player designated by the Coach will indicate to the Referee that his Team is exercising its option and the Referee will report the time-out to the Game Timekeeper who shall be responsible for signalling the termination of the time-out.

(NOTE 1) All players including goalkeepers on the ice at the time of the time-out will be allowed to go to their respective benches. Only one Team is allowed a time-out per stoppage and no time-out will be allowed after a reasonable amount of time has elapsed during a normal stoppage of play.

(NOTE 2) For the purposes of this Rule, a commercial stoppage in play is deemed to be an "official time-out" and not charged to either Team.

Rule 93. Video Goal Judge

The following situations are subject to review by the Video Goal Judge:

(a) Puck crossing the goal line.

(b) Puck in the net prior to the goal frame being dislodged.

(c) Puck in the net prior to, or after expiration of time at the end of the period.

(d) Puck directed into the net by a hand or foot. With the use of a foot/skate, was a distinct kicking motion evident? If so, the apparent goal must be disallowed.

(e) Puck deflected into the net off an Official.

(f) Puck struck with a high-stick, above the height of the crossbar, by an attacking player prior to entering the goal.

(g) To establish the correct time on the official game clock, provided the game time is visible on the Video Goal Judge's monitors.

Notes

Notes

Notes

Notes

Notes

Notes

Notes

Notes

Notes

NHL Schedule, 1999-2000

Game #	Visitor	Home
FRI OCT 1		
1	PIT	DAL
2	NYR	EDM
SAT OCT 2		
3	CAR	BOS
4	TOR	MTL
5	OTT	PHI
6	N.J.	ATL
7	NYI	T.B.
8	WSH	FLA
9	BUF	DET
10	PHX	ST.L.
11	L.A.	NSH
12	ANA	DAL
13	NYR	VAN
14	CGY	S.J.
MON OCT 4		
15	BOS	TOR
16	L.A.	ST.L.
17	CHI	S.J.
TUE OCT 5		
18	OTT	NYR
19	DAL	DET
20	COL	NSH
21	ANA	PHX
WED OCT 6		
22	COL	TOR
23	L.A.	FLA
24	ST.L.	CGY
25	MTL	EDM
26	CHI	VAN
THU OCT 7		
27	BOS	OTT
28	PIT	N.J.
29	CAR	PHI
30	DET	ATL
31	L.A.	T.B.
32	EDM	S.J.
FRI OCT 8		
33	WSH	BUF
34	CAR	NYR

Game #	Visitor	Home
FRI OCT 8		
35	COL	PIT
36	PHX	CHI
37	MTL	CGY
38	DAL	ANA
SAT OCT 9		
39	PHI	BOS
40	TOR	OTT
41	T.B.	N.J.
42	L.A.	WSH
43	BUF	ATL
44	DET	FLA
45	ST.L.	EDM
46	•MTL	VAN
47	DAL	S.J.
SUN OCT 10		
48	•COL	NYI
49	•PHX	NYR
50	NSH	CHI
MON OCT 11		
51	• COL	BOS
52	PHX	BUF
53	NSH	TOR
54	•N.J.	OTT
55	NYR	NYI
56	•CAR	CGY
57	•S.J.	ANA
TUE OCT 12		
58	FLA	MTL
59	PHI	WSH
WED OCT 13		
60	FLA	TOR
61	ANA	N.J.
62	ST.L.	DET
63	S.J.	DAL
64	BOS	COL
65	CAR	EDM
66	CGY	VAN
• *AFTERNOON GAME*		

Game #	Visitor	Home
THU OCT 14		
67	ATL	NYI
68	PIT	NYR
69	MTL	PHI
70	S.J.	NSH
71	OTT	PHX
FRI OCT 15		
72	ANA	T.B.
73	TOR	CHI
74	BOS	DAL
75	L.A.	CGY
76	CAR	VAN
SAT OCT 16		
77	BUF	MTL
78	NYI	N.J.
79	CHI	PIT
80	S.J.	WSH
81	ATL	T.B.
82	ANA	FLA
83	PHI	DET
84	TOR	ST.L.
85	DAL	NSH
86	OTT	COL
87	VAN	CGY
88	L.A.	EDM
89	BOS	PHX
SUN OCT 17		
90	ATL	NYR
91	BUF	PHI
MON OCT 18		
92	NYI	MTL
TUE OCT 19		
93	S.J.	NYR
94	ANA	WSH
95	VAN	T.B.
96	CGY	ST.L.
WED OCT 20		
97	NSH	BUF
98	CAR	TOR
99	COL	MTL
100	NYR	PHI

Game #	Visitor	Home
WED OCT 20		
101	VAN	FLA
102	S.J.	DET
103	EDM	DAL
104	BOS	L.A.
THU OCT 21		
105	COL	OTT
106	ANA	CHI
107	EDM	ST.L.
FRI OCT 22		
108	CAR	BUF
109	PHI	NYR
110	CGY	FLA
112	N.J.	DAL
113	PHX	L.A.
SAT OCT 23		
114	MTL	TOR
115	BUF	OTT
116	VAN	NYI
117	CAR	PIT
118	COL	ATL
119	CGY	T.B.
120	DET	CHI
121	N.J.	ST.L.
122	EDM	NSH
123	WSH	PHX
124	BOS	S.J.
SUN OCT 24		
125	VAN	NYR
126	FLA	PHI
127	BOS	ANA
128	S.J.	L.A.
MON OCT 25		
129	DAL	TOR
TUE OCT 26		
130	VAN	PHI
131	CGY	ATL
132	PHX	EDM
133	WSH	L.A.

Game #	Visitor	Home
WED OCT 27		
134	T.B.	BUF
135	ATL	TOR
136	CHI	MTL
137	ST.L.	N.J.
138	NYI	FLA
139	COL	DET
140	PIT	ANA
THU OCT 28		
141	T.B.	BOS
142	CGY	OTT
143	COL	PHI
144	PHX	VAN
145	PIT	L.A.
146	NSH	S.J.
FRI OCT 29		
147	FLA	BUF
148	N.J.	CAR
149	CHI	DET
150	WSH	ANA
SAT OCT 30		
151	BUF	BOS
152	CGY	TOR
153	NYR	MTL
154	FLA	OTT
155	CAR	NYI
156	N.J.	PHI
157	L.A.	CHI
158	DET	ST.L.
159	T.B.	DAL
160	•PHX	COL
161	NSH	VAN
162	PIT	S.J.
SUN OCT 31		
163	OTT	ATL
164	NSH	EDM
165	PHX	ANA
166	WSH	S.J.
TUE NOV 2		
167	L.A.	PIT
WED NOV 3		
168	MTL	N.J.
169	NYI	NYR
170	OTT	WSH

Game #	Visitor	Home
WED NOV 3		
171	TOR	CAR
172	T.B.	ATL
173	L.A.	DET
174	BUF	DAL
175	ST.L.	COL
176	NSH	CGY
177	FLA	EDM
178	PHI	ANA
179	PHX	S.J.
THU NOV 4		
180	N.J.	BOS
181	PIT	OTT
182	MTL	NYI
183	BUF	CHI
FRI NOV 5		
184	TOR	WSH
185	CAR	DET
186	CHI	NSH
187	NYR	COL
188	ST.L.	EDM
189	FLA	VAN
190	DAL	PHX
191	PHI	S.J.
SAT NOV 6		
192	ATL	BOS
193	NYI	BUF
194	MTL	OTT
195	TOR	N.J.
196	T.B.	PIT
197	FLA	CGY
198	PHI	L.A.
199	DAL	S.J.
SUN NOV 7		
200	WSH	CAR
201	DET	T.B.
202	NYR	CHI
203	ST.L.	VAN
204	EDM	ANA
TUE NOV 9		
205	ANA	TOR
206	PHI	N.J.
207	T.B.	WSH
208	DAL	ST.L.

Game #	Visitor	Home
TUE NOV 9		
209	S.J.	VAN
210	EDM	L.A.
WED NOV 10		
211	BOS	BUF
212	OTT	NYR
213	MTL	PIT
214	NYI	CAR
215	ATL	FLA
WED NOV 10		
216	NSH	CHI
217	DET	DAL
218	S.J.	CGY
219	EDM	PHX
THU NOV 11		
220	TOR	BOS
221	ANA	MTL
222	NSH	OTT
223	CAR	PHI
224	NYR	WSH
225	COL	L.A.
FRI NOV 12		
226	ATL	N.J.
227	BUF	T.B.
228	PIT	DET
229	NYI	CHI
230	EDM	ST.L.
231	VAN	PHX
SAT NOV 13		
232	DET	TOR
233	ATL	MTL
234	ANA	OTT
236	BOS	NYR
237	•S.J.	PHI
238	NSH	PIT
239	N.J.	WSH
240	T.B.	CAR
241	BUF	FLA
242	COL	CGY
SUN NOV 14		
243	EDM	CHI
244	L.A.	PHX
MON NOV 15		
111	ANA	DET
245	S.J.	TOR

Game #	Visitor	Home
MON NOV 15		
246	COL	VAN
TUE NOV 16		
247	S.J.	MTL
248	BUF	DET
249	CGY	PHX
250	CHI	L.A.
WED NOV 17		
251	ST.L.	TOR
252	BOS	N.J.
253	DAL	WSH
254	OTT	CAR
255	T.B.	ATL
256	FLA	COL
257	DET	VAN
258	CGY	ANA
THU NOV 18		
259	NYR	BOS
260	S.J.	OTT
261	DAL	PHI
262	PIT	T.B.
263	FLA	ST.L.
264	MTL	NSH
265	PHX	L.A.
FRI NOV 19		
266	CAR	WSH
267	BUF	ATL
268	NYI	COL
269	DET	CGY
270	CHI	ANA
SAT NOV 20		
271	WSH	BOS
272	ATL	BUF
273	NYR	TOR*
* Hockey Hall of Fame game		
274	•OTT	N.J.
275	T.B.	PHI
276	DAL	CAR
277	PIT	FLA
278	S.J.	ST.L.
279	VAN	NSH
280	DET	EDM
281	CHI	PHX
282	MTL	L.A.

GAME #	VISITOR	HOME
SUN NOV 21		
283	NYI	EDM
MON NOV 22		
284	BOS	CAR
285	VAN	ATL
286	PHI	T.B.
287	NSH	ST.L.
288	COL	DAL
289	MTL	ANA
TUE NOV 23		
290	TOR	PIT
291	L.A.	COL
292	NYI	CGY
293	MTL	S.J.
WED NOV 24		
294	WSH	BUF
295	VAN	CAR
296	NYR	T.B.
297	PHI	FLA
298	ST.L.	DET
299	BOS	NSH
300	L.A.	DAL
WED NOV 24		
301	CHI	EDM
302	N.J.	ANA
THU NOV 25		
303	OTT	ATL
304	CHI	CGY
305	N.J.	PHX
FRI NOV 26		
306	•VAN	BOS
307	ST.L.	BUF
308	•TOR	PHI
309	OTT	PIT
310	NSH	WSH
311	CAR	T.B.
312	NYR	FLA
313	EDM	DET
314	•ANA	DAL
315	COL	PHX
SAT NOV 27		
316	EDM	TOR
317	VAN	MTL
318	WSH	NYI

GAME #	VISITOR	HOME
SAT NOV 27		
319	PIT	CAR
320	ATL	FLA
321	CHI	ST.L.
322	ANA	NSH
323	CGY	COL
324	•S.J.	L.A.
SUN NOV 28		
325	NYI	BOS
326	•PHI	OTT
327	DAL	ATL
328	BUF	T.B.
329	•PHX	DET
330	N.J.	S.J.
MON NOV 29		
331	WSH	TOR
TUE NOV 30		
332	PIT	BUF
333	CHI	OTT
334	DAL	NYI
335	CGY	CAR
336	PHX	NSH
337	COL	VAN
WED DEC 1		
338	DAL	MTL
339	NYR	N.J.
340	S.J.	DET
341	COL	EDM
342	T.B.	ANA
THU DEC 2		
343	PHI	BUF
344	CGY	NYI
345	S.J.	PIT
346	BOS	WSH
347	TOR	CAR
348	NSH	ST.L.
349	EDM	VAN
350	T.B.	PHX
FRI DEC 3		
351	OTT	N.J.
352	MTL	NYR
353	FLA	ATL
354	DET	CHI
355	L.A.	ANA

GAME #	VISITOR	HOME
SAT DEC 4		
356	CHI	BOS
357	NYR	BUF
358	PIT	TOR
359	PHI	MTL
360	DAL	OTT
361	CGY	N.J.
362	ATL	NYI
363	WSH	FLA
364	S.J.	ST.L.
365	DET	NSH
366	CAR	COL
367	VAN	EDM
368	ANA	PHX
369	T.B.	L.A.
SUN DEC 5		
370	ST.L.	PHI
MON DEC 6		
371	BUF	TOR
372	CGY	NYR
373	NSH	ATL
374	EDM	CHI
375	PHX	DAL
376	VAN	COL
377	T.B.	S.J.
TUE DEC 7		
378	CGY	MTL
379	PIT	N.J.
380	NYI	WSH
381	CAR	ST.L.
WED DEC 8		
382	OTT	BUF
383	EDM	NYR
384	NSH	DET
385	CAR	DAL
386	FLA	PHX
387	VAN	ANA
388	ATL	L.A.
389	COL	S.J.
THU DEC 9		
390	EDM	BOS
391	MTL	NYI
392	TOR	PHI
393	WSH	PIT
394	N.J.	CHI

GAME #	VISITOR	HOME
FRI DEC 10		
395	CHI	BUF
396	CAR	T.B.
397	L.A.	DET
398	ST.L.	NSH
399	FLA	DAL
400	VAN	CGY
401	COL	ANA
402	ATL	S.J.
SAT DEC 11		
403	DET	BOS
404	PHI	TOR
405	L.A.	MTL
406	•NYI	OTT
407	•EDM	N.J.
408	PHX	PIT
409	DAL	ST.L.
410	FLA	NSH
SUN DEC 12		
411	CGY	CHI
412	COL	VAN
413	ATL	ANA
MON DEC 13		
414	PHX	BOS
415	OTT	TOR
416	MTL	WSH
TUE DEC 14		
417	PHI	BUF
418	L.A.	N.J.
419	EDM	NYI
420	BOS	PIT
421	NSH	T.B.
422	CGY	ST.L.
423	CHI	S.J.
WED DEC 15		
424	NYI	TOR
425	L.A.	NYR
426	PIT	CAR
427	WSH	ATL
428	NSH	FLA
429	EDM	DET
430	CGY	DAL
431	ANA	COL

• *AFTERNOON GAME*

Game #	Visitor	Home
THU DEC 16		
432	N.J.	MTL
433	PHX	PHI
434	OTT	VAN
FRI DEC 17		
435	FLA	BUF
436	WSH	NYR
437	BOS	ATL
438	COL	DET
439	DAL	EDM
440	CHI	ANA
SAT DEC 18		
441	MTL	TOR
442	WSH	N.J.
443	BUF	NYI
444	T.B.	PHI
445	FLA	PIT
446	ATL	CAR
447	BOS	ST.L.
448	COL	NSH
449	OTT	CGY
450	DAL	VAN
451	CHI	L.A.
SUN DEC 19		
452	N.J.	NYI
453	T.B.	NYR
454	NSH	PHI
455	OTT	EDM
456	•S.J.	PHX
457	DET	ANA
MON DEC 20		
458	PIT	MTL
459	COL	CAR
460	TOR	FLA
461	DET	S.J.
TUE DEC 21		
462	NSH	BOS
463	PIT	NYI
464	BUF	NYR
465	TOR	T.B.
466	DAL	CGY
467	WSH	EDM
468	ST.L.	PHX

Game #	Visitor	Home
WED DEC 22		
469	PHI	N.J.
471	ATL	FLA
472	WSH	VAN
473	PHX	ANA
474	L.A.	S.J.
THU DEC 23		
475	MTL	BOS
476	COL	BUF
477	N.J.	TOR
478	CAR	OTT
479	NYR	NYI
480	ATL	PHI
481	T.B.	PIT
482	DAL	CHI
483	ST.L.	NSH
484	EDM	CGY
SUN DEC 26		
485	• N.J.	NYR
486	FLA	CAR
487	T.B.	ATL
488	PIT	CHI
489	NSH	ST.L.
490	CGY	VAN
491	PHX	L.A.
492	•ANA	S.J.
MON DEC 27		
493	MTL	OTT
494	BUF	N.J.
495	BOS	NYI
496	CHI	WSH
497	FLA	T.B.
498	ATL	DET
499	S.J.	DAL
500	ST.L.	COL
501	PHI	CGY
502	ANA	EDM
TUE DEC 28		
503	DET	BUF
504	CAR	NSH
505	NYR	PHX
WED DEC 29		
506	OTT	MTL
507	BOS	N.J.

Game #	Visitor	Home
WED DEC 29		
508	TOR	NYI
509	PIT	WSH
510	NYR	DAL
511	L.A.	COL
512	ANA	CGY
513	PHI	VAN
THU DEC 30		
514	BOS	OTT
515	NYI	PIT
516	FLA	CHI
517	S.J.	ST.L.
518	ATL	NSH
519	EDM	L.A.
FRI DEC 31		
520	CHI	DET
521	ANA	DAL
SAT JAN 1		
522	N.J.	BOS
523	TOR	BUF
524	ST.L.	WSH
525	CAR	ATL
526	•T.B.	FLA
527	•S.J.	NSH
528	EDM	PHX
SUN JAN 2		
529	NYR	MTL
530	•PHI	NYI
531	DET	PIT
532	S.J.	CHI
533	•VAN	CGY
MON JAN 3		
534	BUF	TOR
535	•N.J.	OTT
536	ST.L.	NYR
537	L.A.	DAL
538	EDM	COL
TUE JAN 4		
539	ATL	BUF
540	BOS	NYI
541	MTL	WSH
542	OTT	CAR
543	PHX	DET
544	L.A.	ST.L.

Game #	Visitor	Home
WED JAN 5		
545	TOR	NYR
546	N.J.	PIT
547	NSH	DAL
548	CGY	COL
549	S.J.	EDM
550	T.B.	VAN
551	FLA	ANA
THU JAN 6		
552	CAR	BOS
553	N.J.	BUF
554	PHX	OTT
555	NYI	PHI
556	WSH	ATL
557	NSH	DET
558	CGY	CHI
559	MTL	ST.L.
560	FLA	L.A.
FRI JAN 7		
561	TOR	PIT
562	ANA	CAR
563	VAN	DAL
564	MTL	COL
565	T.B.	EDM
SAT JAN 8		
566	NYI	BOS
567	NYR	TOR
568	BUF	OTT
569	PHX	N.J.
570	PIT	PHI
571	ATL	WSH
572	ANA	DET
573	VAN	ST.L.
574	CHI	NSH
575	T.B.	CGY
576	FLA	S.J.
SUN JAN 9		
577	NYR	CAR
578	COL	CHI
MON JAN 10		
579	PHX	NYI
TUE JAN 11		
580	TOR	BOS
581	DET	MTL

Game #	Visitor	Home
TUE JAN 11		
582	PHI	CAR
583	N.J.	T.B.
584	NSH	COL
585	DAL	EDM
586	OTT	L.A.
587	ST.L.	S.J.
WED JAN 12		
588	WSH	ATL
589	NYI	FLA
590	VAN	CHI
591	DAL	CGY
592	PIT	PHX
593	OTT	ANA
THU JAN 13		
594	BUF	BOS
595	NYI	T.B.
596	CHI	DET
597	VAN	NSH
598	PIT	COL
599	ST.L.	L.A.
FRI JAN 14		
600	MTL	BUF
601	WSH	N.J.
602	PHI	ATL
603	CAR	FLA
604	TOR	EDM
605	ST.L.	ANA
SAT JAN 15		
606	BOS	MTL
607	•NYR	NYI
608	N.J.	PHI
609	FLA	T.B.
610	PIT	NSH
611	CHI	COL
612	TOR	CGY
613	DAL	VAN
614	ANA	PHX
615	L.A.	S.J.
SUN JAN 16		
616	•ATL	NYR
617	•OTT	WSH
618	DET	EDM

Game #	Visitor	Home
MON JAN 17		
619	•ATL	BOS
620	CAR	N.J.
621	•OTT	NYI
622	•WSH	T.B.
623	•PHI	FLA
624	•S.J.	CHI
625	PHX	COL
626	TOR	VAN
627	BUF	ANA
TUE JAN 18		
628	CAR	NYR
629	PHX	NSH
630	DET	CGY
631	BUF	L.A.
WED JAN 19		
632	NYI	MTL
633	CHI	N.J.
634	ST.L.	PIT
635	BOS	ATL
636	WSH	FLA
637	S.J.	COL
638	CGY	EDM
639	DET	VAN
640	DAL	ANA
THU JAN 20		
641	OTT	PHI
642	NYR	CAR
643	BOS	T.B.
644	BUF	PHX
645	DAL	L.A.
FRI JAN 21		
646	NYI	N.J.
647	FLA	ATL
648	ST.L.	CHI
649	NSH	CGY
650	COL	ANA
SAT JAN 22		
651	WSH	TOR
652	PIT	MTL
653	DET	OTT
654	T.B.	NYI
655	•BUF	CAR
656	BOS	FLA

Game #	Visitor	Home
SAT JAN 22		
657	NYR	ST.L.
658	VAN	EDM
659	ANA	S.J.
SUN JAN 23		
660	PHI	PIT
661	DAL	CHI
662	NSH	VAN
663	S.J.	PHX
664	•COL	L.A.
MON JAN 24		
665	CGY	BOS
666	OTT	TOR
667	T.B.	WSH
668	MTL	CAR
669	NYR	ATL
670	NSH	EDM
TUE JAN 25		
671	T.B.	BUF
672	NYR	PIT
673	PHX	CAR
674	EDM	VAN
675	COL	S.J.
WED JAN 26		
676	ST.L.	OTT
677	CGY	WSH
678	PHX	ATL
679	N.J.	FLA
680	TOR	DET
681	L.A.	DAL
682	NYI	ANA
THU JAN 27		
683	MTL	BOS
684	TOR	NYR
685	FLA	PHI
686	ATL	PIT
687	COL	CHI
688	L.A.	NSH
FRI JAN 28		
689	OTT	BUF
690	PHX	WSH
691	N.J.	CAR
692	EDM	T.B.
693	CGY	DET

Game #	Visitor	Home
FRI JAN 28		
694	ST.L.	DAL
695	S.J.	VAN
SAT JAN 29		
696	BUF	BOS
697	L.A.	TOR
698	•PHI	MTL
699	NYR	OTT
700	ANA	PIT
701	ATL	T.B.
702	EDM	FLA
703	N.J.	DET
704	COL	ST.L.
706	NYI	S.J.
SUN JAN 30		
707	•CAR	MTL
708	•PHI	WSH
709	CHI	VAN
MON JAN 31		
710	ANA	BOS
711	NSH	NYR
712	PIT	ATL
713	EDM	DAL
714	DET	PHX
715	NYI	L.A.
TUE FEB 1		
716	ANA	BUF
717	BOS	OTT
718	WSH	PIT
719	FLA	CAR
720	TOR	T.B.
721	VAN	COL
722	ST.L.	CGY
723	PHX	S.J.
WED FEB 2		
724	NSH	NYI
725	N.J.	NYR
726	MTL	FLA
727	ATL	DAL
728	CHI	EDM
THU FEB 3		
729	TOR	BOS
730	OTT	BUF

• *AFTERNOON GAME*

Game #	Visitor	Home
731	NSH	N.J.

THU FEB 3

Game #	Visitor	Home
732	ANA	PHI
733	NYI	PIT
734	CAR	WSH
735	NYR	ATL
736	MTL	T.B.
737	S.J.	COL
738	CHI	CGY
739	ST.L.	VAN
740	DAL	PHX
741	DET	L.A.

SUN FEB 6
NHL All-Star Game–Toronto

TUE FEB 8

Game #	Visitor	Home
742	WSH	BOS
743	EDM	MTL
744	CAR	NYI
745	N.J.	NYR
746	S.J.	T.B.
747	ST.L.	DET
748	BUF	COL
749	ANA	L.A.

WED FEB 9

Game #	Visitor	Home
750	PHI	TOR
751	NYR	N.J.
752	ATL	PIT
753	S.J.	FLA
754	CGY	VAN
755	L.A.	PHX
756	DAL	ANA

THU FEB 10

Game #	Visitor	Home
757	WSH	MTL
758	T.B.	NYI
759	EDM	PHI
760	DET	ST.L.
761	BUF	NSH
762	CGY	COL

FRI FEB 11

Game #	Visitor	Home
763	FLA	OTT
764	BOS	NYR
765	EDM	PIT
766	S.J.	ATL
767	DAL	L.A.

SAT FEB 12

Game #	Visitor	Home
768	FLA	BOS
769	VAN	TOR
770	OTT	MTL
771	PIT	NYI
772	•BUF	PHI
773	CHI	ATL
774	CAR	T.B.
775	ANA	ST.L.
776	WSH	NSH
777	CGY	PHX

SUN FEB 13

Game #	Visitor	Home
778	•EDM	BUF
779	•S.J.	N.J.
780	NYI	NYR
781	WSH	DAL
782	DET	COL

MON FEB 14

Game #	Visitor	Home
783	CAR	TOR
784	FLA	MTL
785	VAN	PIT
786	ANA	CHI
787	DET	PHX
788	CGY	L.A.

TUE FEB 15

Game #	Visitor	Home
789	CAR	OTT
790	PHI	N.J.
791	S.J.	NYI
792	COL	WSH
793	NYR	T.B.
794	ATL	ST.L.
795	EDM	NSH

WED FEB 16

Game #	Visitor	Home
796	BOS	TOR
797	BUF	PIT
798	MTL	ATL
799	NYR	FLA
800	VAN	DET
801	L.A.	CHI
802	NSH	DAL
803	CGY	ANA

THU FEB 17

Game #	Visitor	Home
804	VAN	BUF
805	T.B.	OTT

THU FEB 17

Game #	Visitor	Home
806	COL	N.J.
807	NYI	PHI
808	MTL	CAR

FRI FEB 18

Game #	Visitor	Home
809	COL	NYR
810	L.A.	DET
811	WSH	CHI
812	ST.L.	NSH
813	PHX	DAL
814	EDM	CGY
815	S.J.	ANA

SAT FEB 19

Game #	Visitor	Home
816	L.A.	BUF
817	TOR	MTL
818	•VAN	OTT
819	•NYI	N.J.
820	WSH	PHI
821	T.B.	CAR
822	PIT	FLA
823	CGY	EDM

SUN FEB 20

Game #	Visitor	Home
824	PHI	NYR
825	•DET	CHI
826	•DAL	COL
827	ATL	PHX

MON FEB 21

Game #	Visitor	Home
828	N.J.	BUF
829	•DET	NYI
830	•NYR	CAR
831	PIT	T.B.
832	•OTT	FLA
833	DAL	NSH
834	L.A.	EDM
835	BOS	VAN
836	ST.L.	ANA

TUE FEB 22

Game #	Visitor	Home
837	PHX	MTL
838	PIT	NYR
839	CHI	PHI
840	ATL	COL

WED FEB 23

Game #	Visitor	Home
841	PHX	TOR
842	FLA	WSH

WED FEB 23

Game #	Visitor	Home
843	DAL	DET
844	NSH	CHI
845	L.A.	CGY
846	BOS	EDM
847	VAN	ANA
848	ST.L.	S.J.

THU FEB 24

Game #	Visitor	Home
849	N.J.	MTL
850	PIT	PHI
851	FLA	CAR
852	OTT	T.B.

FRI FEB 25

Game #	Visitor	Home
853	NYR	BUF
854	TOR	N.J.
855	BOS	WSH
856	NYI	DET
857	COL	ST.L.
858	CHI	DAL
859	PHX	CGY
860	ATL	EDM
861	L.A.	VAN

SAT FEB 26

Game #	Visitor	Home
862	BUF	TOR
863	WSH	MTL
864	NYR	OTT
865	PHI	NYI
866	BOS	PIT
867	CAR	FLA
868	T.B.	NSH
869	ATL	CGY
870	L.A.	S.J.

SUN FEB 27

Game #	Visitor	Home
871	MTL	N.J.
872	T.B.	DET
873	•CHI	ST.L.
874	COL	DAL
875	PHX	VAN
876	EDM	ANA

MON FEB 28

Game #	Visitor	Home
877	WSH	NYI
878	OTT	PIT
879	BUF	FLA

GAME #VISITOR HOME	GAME #VISITOR HOME	GAME #VISITOR HOME	GAME #VISITOR HOME
TUE FEB 29	**SUN MAR 5**	**SAT MAR 11**	**FRI MAR 17**
880 OTT BOS	918 DET DAL	956 •ANA ST.L.	993 NSH PHX
881 TOR ATL	919 N.J. CGY	957 VAN PHX	994 S.J. ANA
882 PHI ST.L.	920 NSH ANA	958 CGY L.A.	995 ST.L. L.A.
883 N.J. NSH	**MON MAR 6**	**SUN MAR 12**	**SAT MAR 18**
884 EDM COL	921 OTT BOS	959 •NYI BUF	996 •PIT BOS
885 VAN L.A.	922 ATL MTL	960 •ATL CAR	997 ATL TOR
886 ANA S.J.	923 TOR VAN	961 CHI T.B.	998 CAR MTL
WED MAR 1	924 NYR S.J.	962 •EDM NSH	999 FLA NYI
887 BUF NYR	**TUE MAR 7**	963 •ST.L. DAL	1000 •NYR PHI
888 WSH T.B.	925 FLA WSH	964 PHI COL	1001 •DAL CHI
889 TOR FLA	926 PHX ST.L.	**MON MAR 13**	1002 •DET COL
890 MTL CHI	927 CHI NSH	965 DAL NYR	1003 BUF CGY
891 PHI DAL	928 COL CGY	966 N.J. PIT	1004 OTT VAN
892 PIT CGY	929 TOR EDM	967 EDM ATL	**SUN MAR 19**
893 CAR PHX	930 DET L.A.	968 PHI PHX	1005 FLA N.J.
THU MAR 2	**WED MAR 8**	969 VAN L.A.	1006 •BOS PHI
894 OTT NYI	931 BOS BUF	970 CGY S.J.	1007 NYR PIT
895 ST.L. ATL	932 MTL PIT	**TUE MAR 14**	1008 •T.B. WSH
896 N.J. COL	933 CHI CAR	971 T.B. MTL	1009 •S.J. DAL
897 ANA VAN	934 PHI T.B.	972 NSH DET	1010 CGY EDM
898 CAR L.A.	935 VAN DAL	973 ANA COL	1011 DET ANA
899 NSH S.J.	936 NYR ANA	**WED MAR 15**	1012 NSH L.A.
FRI MAR 3	937 DET S.J.	974 CHI TOR	**MON MAR 20**
900 FLA NYR	**THU MAR 9**	975 DAL N.J.	1013 MTL BUF
901 DET WSH	938 PIT OTT	976 T.B. NYR	1014 WSH ST.L.
902 T.B. CHI	939 WSH PHI	977 NYI WSH	1015 VAN COL
903 ANA CGY	941 TOR CGY	978 EDM CAR	**TUE MAR 21**
904 DAL PHX	942 NYI PHX	979 OTT CGY	1016 T.B. BOS
SAT MAR 4	943 NYR L.A.	980 ST.L. PHX	1017 ATL OTT
905 •PHI BOS	**FRI MAR 10**	981 L.A. ANA	1018 CAR N.J.
906 MTL TOR	944 MTL BUF	982 BUF S.J.	1019 PIT NYI
907 ATL OTT	945 BOS CAR	**THU MAR 16**	1020 FLA NYR
908 •BUF NYI	946 N.J. ATL	983 MTL PHI	1021 PHI NSH
909 ST.L. FLA	947 FLA T.B.	984 FLA PIT	1022 CHI PHX
910 T.B. COL	948 DET NSH	985 NYI ATL	1023 ANA L.A.
911 PIT EDM	949 NYI DAL	986 TOR DET	**WED MAR 22**
912 N.J. VAN	950 COL EDM	987 BOS CHI	1024 NYI TOR
913 NSH L.A.	**SAT MAR 11**	988 NSH COL	1025 ST.L. CAR
914 CAR S.J.	951 BOS MTL	989 BUF VAN	1026 MTL ATL
SUN MAR 5	952 TOR OTT	**FRI MAR 17**	1027 CGY DET
915 NYI PHI	953 NYR PIT	990 T.B. N.J.	1028 ANA EDM
916 •BUF WSH	954 N.J. WSH	991 CAR WSH	1029 VAN S.J.
917 •PHX CHI	955 CHI FLA	992 OTT EDM	
			• *AFTERNOON GAME*

Game #	Visitor	Home
THU MAR 23		
1030	FLA	BOS
1031	CGY	BUF
1032	TOR	OTT
1033	WSH	NYR
1034	L.A.	PHI
1035	DET	NSH
1036	COL	PHX
FRI MAR 24		
1037	N.J.	NYI
1038	PIT	ATL
1039	ST.L.	T.B.
1040	CHI	DAL
1041	ANA	VAN
1042	PHX	S.J.
SAT MAR 25		
1043	•L.A.	BOS
1044	N.J.	TOR
1045	WSH	OTT
1046	MTL	FLA
1047	CGY	NSH
1048	VAN	EDM
SUN MAR 26		
1049	•PIT	PHI
1050	•NYI	CAR
1051	L.A.	ATL
1052	MTL	T.B.
1053	•NYR	DET
1054	•ST.L.	CHI
1055	•COL	DAL
1056	PHX	ANA
MON MAR 27		
1057	DET	NYR
1058	BUF	CAR
1059	CHI	COL
1060	EDM	S.J.

Game #	Visitor	Home
TUE MAR 28		
1061	PHI	OTT
1062	N.J.	PIT
1063	ATL	WSH
1064	DAL	T.B.
1065	NYI	NSH
WED MAR 29		
1066	BOS	MTL
1067	NSH	CAR
1068	DAL	FLA
1069	VAN	DET
1070	TOR	ST.L.
1071	EDM	COL
1072	S.J.	L.A.
THU MAR 30		
1073	ST.L.	BOS
1074	PIT	WSH
1075	OTT	T.B.
1076	TOR	CHI
FRI MAR 31		
1077	CAR	BUF
1078	ATL	N.J.
1079	OTT	FLA
1080	VAN	NSH
1081	PHX	CGY
SAT APR 1		
1082	•NYR	BOS
1083	BUF	MTL
1084	•CHI	NYI
1085	•PHI	PIT
1086	TOR	WSH
1087	T.B.	FLA
1088	•DET	ST.L.
1089	S.J.	CGY
1090	PHX	EDM
1091	•ANA	L.A.

Game #	Visitor	Home
SUN APR 2		
1092	•PHI	CAR
1093	•NYI	ATL
1094	N.J.	T.B.
1095	MTL	DET
1096	•VAN	CHI
1097	•OTT	ST.L.
1098	•DAL	COL
MON APR 3		
1099	TOR	BUF
1100	CAR	PIT
1101	NYR	WSH
1102	N.J.	FLA
1103	CGY	DAL
1104	S.J.	EDM
1105	L.A.	PHX
1106	NSH	ANA
TUE APR 4		
1107	WSH	OTT
1108	PHI	ATL
1109	BOS	T.B.
WED APR 5		
1110	PIT	TOR
1111	MTL	NYR
1112	BOS	FLA
1113	ANA	CHI
1114	CGY	ST.L.
1115	COL	EDM
1116	L.A.	VAN
1117	NSH	PHX
1118	DAL	S.J.
THU APR 6		
1119	T.B.	MTL
1120	NYI	OTT
1121	BUF	N.J.
1122	ATL	PHI

Game #	Visitor	Home
FRI APR 7		
1123	PIT	BUF
1124	TOR	NYI
1125	WSH	DET
1126	CHI	ST.L.
1127	ANA	NSH
1128	COL	CGY
1129	EDM	VAN
1130	S.J.	PHX
1131	DAL	L.A.
SAT APR 8		
1132	T.B.	TOR
1133	OTT	MTL
1134	•FLA	N.J.
1135	•BOS	PHI
1136	•CAR	ATL
1137	EDM	CGY
SUN APR 9		
1138	PIT	BOS
1139	T.B.	OTT
1140	•FLA	NYI
1141	•PHI	NYR
1142	•BUF	WSH
1143	•ATL	CAR
1144	•ST.L.	CHI
1145	•PHX	DAL
1146	•DET	COL
1147	•L.A.	ANA
1148	VAN	S.J.